GOODBYE
to the
LOW PROFILE

GOODBYE to the LOW PROFILE

The Art of Creative Confrontation

HERB SCHMERTZ
and
WILLIAM NOVAK

MERCURY BOOKS · LONDON

First published in the USA by Little, Brown & Co. 1986
This edition published in 1986
by the Mercury Books Division of
W. H. Allen & Co. Plc
44 Hill Street, London W1X 8LB

Photoset in Concorde by
Phoenix Photosetting, Chatham, Kent
Printed and bound in Great Britain by
Mackays of Chatham Ltd, Chatham, Kent

British Library Cataloguing in Publication Data

Schmertz, Herb
Goodbye to the low profile: the art of
creative confrontation.
1. Communication in management
2. Interpersonal communication
I. Title II. Novak, William
302.3'46'024658 HD30.3

ISBN 1–85251–000–5

For Susie

Contents

Acknowledgments

Without Bill Novak's long hours of patience, incisive questioning, and brilliant organizing of my thoughts, views, and opinions, this book would not have been possible.

Bill Phillips's editing pushed me to improvements and refinements beyond what I thought I was capable of achieving.

Esther Newberg, my agent, deserves major thanks, not only for arranging for the publication of this book but also for her constructive criticism and support.

My thanks also to Jim Dulicai, who helped me at the beginning to develop the concept for this book and who regularly and diligently provided perceptive comments.

Finally, thanks to my friends Rawleigh Warner, Jr., and Bill Tavoulareas, from whom I learned so much and who made it all possible.

Foreword

by Carol Friend, MIPR
Managing Director, Pielle Public Relations and
1986 President of The Institute of Public Relations

Herb Schmertz has been described to me by North American public relations professionals as a high-calibre, quality corporate PR man. He has a non-traditional background and the most personable of presentation styles, good management skills and a natural talent for communication. Everything I have read in this book leads me to concur with that view.

In his easy, readable style, Herb Schmertz tells and shows what the role of public relations as a management function should be. Its function, he says, and I agree, is to present the organisation's personality and its philosophy to its various publics. This management role and its implementation, he asserts, should not be kept in an airtight box of specialists but, for maximum effectiveness, should be an integrated part of senior management thinking and action – and so say I.

Like many business writers with a popular appeal, our author makes some dramatic statements to get his points across. Taken out of context, these could lead the speed reader to think that Schmertz, like Townsend in *Up The Organisation*, believes that public relations professionals are an unnecessary luxury; that every employee, product or service is your only required public relations tool.

In fact, as every thinking manager will realise, he is no more saying this than any rational, high-calibre executive would suggest disbanding the company's financial team because financial responsibilities are a part of every management function.

This is a book which all managers who work with internal or

external public relations resources should read. It will give them an insight into the scope of a valuable public relations input they should be seeking and getting; demonstrating that there should be a whole world of public relations beyond the publicity.

It is also a book for managers who do not employ any professional public relations thinking in their work. It will begin to show this unenlightened group what they are missing.

All senior managers who relegate public relations to middle or junior executive levels should use this book to learn better. If you don't your competitors might and that can only be to your commercial disadvantage. The student of public relations should read it to develop an insight into good quality corporate thinking.

This is, of course, a book of American experience but while the context and operational criteria may be different on this side of the Atlantic, the basic concepts and techniques remain relevant. Use the political references as interesting comments on the American way but for '60 minutes' read 'That's Life', 'World in Action' or 'TV Eye'; for 'op-ed ads' read 'corporate issue advertising'.

Goodbye to the Low Profile is a good read. Nothing too revolutionary, but plenty of good sense and useful reminders. Try it as your reading on a long journey as a panacea to the guilt complex that comes with not working while travelling. It is likely to make a useful contribution to the development of many a professional manager.

ONE

What to Do When *60 Minutes* Calls

YOU'RE SITTING IN your office one day, and the telephone rings. 'Hello,' says the caller. 'This is Mike Wallace of *Sixty Minutes*. I'd like to interview you for a story we're working on.' Or suppose the caller is a reporter from the *Wall Street Journal* who asks you to respond to some highly damaging charges about your company. Or perhaps it's a friend who's just heard on the radio that a United States senator has charged that your company doesn't really care about the welfare of its customers.

In any of these cases, would you know how to respond?

If you're like most corporate executives, the answer is probably no. But if you have any intention of rising to the top levels of management, you had better learn what to do in these and similar situations. Whatever type of company or organization you work for, the odds are good that the leadership skills you have shown so far, while sufficient to gain your supervisor's attention, are not the skills you will need to succeed at the top. As good as you may be at number-crunching, organizing, and motivating, you will have to break out of that narrow mould to learn a new and broader set of tools and techniques.

To put it another way, you've probably been trained to deal only with domestic matters – with problems inside the corporation. What you need now is a crash course in the business equivalent of foreign affairs.

These days, more than ever before, business leaders and their advisers are being called upon to solve a wide range of problems – not only traditional business problems like selling and marketing, but other problems, too, involving people from the outside world with an astounding variety of interests and viewpoints. No matter where you work, the chances are that the top management of your company is facing – or will face – a variety of problems with government and with the media, not to mention special-interest groups and other lobbies. Until recently, dealing with important groups and individuals outside of one's own industry was the sole concern of the PR department. These days, however, it's a number-one priority for top management.

To solve these and other challenges, you'll need far more than a public-relations handbook. What you need, and what you're about to get, is a tool for dealing creatively and successfully with the public. This book is intended to be a passport to the world outside your organization and beyond your own area of technical competence.

No book – not even this one – can turn you into the chairman of the board or even the vice-president for public affairs. Only you can do that for yourself. But I will suggest some specific skills that you can develop with regard to government, the arts, and, especially, the media – outward-looking skills that should generate handsome dividends both to you and to your company in the years ahead.

Why are these skills so important? Because more than ever before, corporations operate in the public arena. Their success is determined not only by their performance in the marketplace, but also by what the marketplace – the public, in other words – thinks about them. Or, more accurately, by what the various publics in our society think about them, because a modern corporation actually deals with many interrelated sub-publics. There's the federal government in Washington, including the White House, the Congress, and the government agencies. There are state governments and local communities. There are television networks, magazines and newspapers, consumers and other special-interest groups, and many more.

Public affairs, then, is a critically important part of management – far too important to be left to the public-affairs professionals. In the final analysis, a company's dealings with the public are only as good – or as bad – as its line management. Every top manager should understand the principles of good public relations, while those who aspire to the role of public-relations advisers must be prepared not only to provide specific solutions to particular problems, but also to act as mentors in the continuing education of the top brass.

Let's look at some specific situations that are typical of the problems discussed in this book.

Suppose Congress has passed legislation that unfairly discriminates against your industry, products, or operations. If you were in a position of leadership, how would you go about getting the matter rectified? Would you pick up the phone and call a representative or a senator? If so, would it be a legislator who represents the state where your company is located? Or a member of the congressional committee that approved the legislation? And if you were invited to visit a particular congressman or senator, how would you prepare for that meeting? And what kind of reception could you expect when you got there?

Or suppose you were summoned to testify at a congressional-committee hearing. Who, if anyone, should come with you? How should you prepare for your ordeal? What steps should you take if you know, for example, that the committee chairman opposes your views on the issue under discussion?

Or let's say that you're a public-relations specialist, and a prominent politician publicly attacks your company. How should you respond? What advice would you give to the chairman? Should he say nothing in the hope that the whole affair will blow over, that today's newspaper story is tomorrow's trash? Should either of you come out immediately with a strong rebuttal? Should you call a news conference to discuss your views?

And what if – as happened to my company – the politician who launches the attack happens to be the president of the United States? Should your response be any different?

Or take the whole vexing issue of political-campaign financing. In view of the brouhaha over political-action committees (PACs), should your company be contributing to them? If you do, what kind of response can you expect? Are there other acceptable ways to encourage a representative or a senator to hear your views? Should you use them? And if so, when?

Or what about the news media? If you're like most executives, you have been trained to think that dealing with the press is the job of the public-relations team, that they're the ones who should either talk to reporters on your behalf or say 'no comment' if you'd rather not make a statement. If that's your impression, then you really need this book. Members of the press won't always be satisfied with your PR person's comments – and neither should you. If you're going to be a leader, then you personally need to establish a rapport with the press. When the moment of crisis arrives – and it almost always does, somewhere along the line – reporters inevitably want to speak to the people at the top. If that's where you aim to be, wouldn't you be a lot better off in that moment of crisis if the press has already come to know you in a less stressful situation?

Your phone rings: it's Mike Wallace again. You didn't know what to say when he called an hour ago, so now he's back. He says that your company has been accused of wrongdoing, and that one of your critics is all set to present a lurid account of the way you have misbehaved. 'Of course,' Mike assures you, 'we want to be fair. We want to hear your side of the story.'

What should you do? Do you say that the whole thing is ridiculous and that *60 Minutes* should find better stories to cover? Do you say, 'Certainly, I'll be glad to tell you our side of the story. Come right over, and I'll be happy to answer all of your questions.'

If you're under the impression that either of these responses is adequate, then you've got a lot to learn about media relations. During the course of this book, I'll have plenty to say about dealing with *60 Minutes* and other shows of that kind.

Or suppose that you turn on the TV news, or open your newspaper, only to find that some reporter has done a hatchet job on your company – or perhaps on your entire industry. What should you do? Write a letter of complaint to the TV network? Send a letter to the editor of the newspaper? Or are there other ways of setting the record straight or of putting the heat on a misinformed reporter?

Or take a problem that my own company, Mobil Oil, had to face back in the energy crisis of 1973–74. In those days, there was a persistent rumour that oil tankers were waiting in New York and other harbours for the price of crude to go up before discharging their cargoes. We knew for a fact that no such tankers existed. So did the Coast Guard – and they said so. We knew that the idea made no sense, because the price of oil had been set by government regulation before our tankers were even loaded. And yet the story was still page-one news and commanded widespread belief.

What would you have done to dispel the rumours? I'll tell you what we did, and I'll also tell you – with hindsight – what we should have done if we had fully realized the extent of the emotional climate in which that accusation was made.

Switching to another issue entirely, what about corporate philanthropy? Should your company give away money to worthy causes? Is Milton Friedman right in believing that 'corporations have no money to give anyone,' and that the sole responsibility of publicly-held corporations is to make money for their shareholders? On the other hand, aren't there good, pragmatic reasons for your company to be doing well by doing good? I believe there are, and I hope to convince you that an insular approach leads not only to bad PR, but also to bad business.

In dealing with these and other problems, I rely on two basic tools. The first tool is *confrontation*, and I'll have a lot more to say about that later on. My second tool is *creativity*.

I realize that most people think that confrontation is something to be avoided at all costs, but I disagree. '*Confront*,' says my dictionary, means 'to stand or meet, face to face.' I take this to mean that confrontation doesn't have to be abrasive or rude or unpleasant, and that it can just as easily be polite and good-humoured. But you can't win your battles by running away from them. You have to get out there and meet your critics head-on. They will respect you for it, and you will have a better chance of getting your message across.

How will you, as a corporate leader, confront your company's opponents? Here, too, the myths abound: The less the company says, the better. The company should speak only through its press-relations department. The company spokesman can issue a statement only after the top executives have approved every word.

Believe me, it doesn't work that way. In the goldfish bowl that is modern corporate life, top management is highly visible. As a result, today's corporate leader must have a deep knowledge of public issues and well-honed communications skills.

In other words, if you aspire to a place at the top, it will help you immeasurably if you are seen as intellectually entitled to have your views taken seriously on important public issues. As a leader, you will become the object of public attention simply by virtue of the power of your institution. But getting attention isn't the same as being taken seriously. You may find yourself at dinner one evening with a senator, two members of the House, a couple of reporters, and a prominent banker who suddenly turns to you and asks, 'Well, what do *you* think the government should do about the balance-of-trade deficit?' An effective leader is able to answer an unexpected and complex question with both insight and confidence.

To be successful as an industrial statesman, then, you have to earn the right to be taken seriously. You will probably have to broaden your horizons, especially through reading a wide spectrum of books and periodicals. You must be familiar with recent political history, foreign affairs, and economics. You should know the names and identities of the key players in Congress, the major staff members in the White House, the important journalists, the editors of the major newspapers, and the presidents of the network news departments. You should feel comfortable in drawing-room conversation about the issues of the day with your counterparts from other industries – and, more important, from other sectors of society.

While these expectations may sound lofty, let's keep in mind that labour leaders have routinely demonstrated these skills, despite the fact that very few of them have ever attended the 'right' schools. But the ingredients for leadership in a labour union include the ability to articulate positions, to debate management, and to interact with other political groups. Isn't it time that management took a page from their book?

To succeed as a leader, you must also be able to speak on your feet in a clear, concise, and convincing way – and without notes. There's no shortcut; it simply takes practice. Lee Iacocca wasn't much of a public speaker when he started out, but after a few sessions at the Dale Carnegie Institute he began to unleash his great potential as an orator. If you want to be recognized as a leader among your employees, not to mention other audiences, you must have the ability to stand up and talk about the business without a text. If you're reading, you're more or less admitting that somebody else wrote what you're saying.

At the same time, there will be more formal occasions when reading from a prepared text is entirely appropriate. Your challenge then will be to read in a way that makes those remarks your own – and keeps your audience awake and engaged.

The ability to confront your opponents also implies a knowledge of debating skills, including some familiarity with your opponent's positions, and, even more important, an ability to really listen to what your opponent is saying. Listening is not a passive act; whenever you're involved in a negotiation, a debate, or even just a meeting with a colleague, always pay close attention to what the other guy is saying. This may sound obvious, but it's not always easy. Most people allow their mind to wander, or else they concentrate on what they're going to say when the other guy is finished.

What should you be listening for? Inconsistencies, contradictions, errors, and examples that are not altogether convincing. You should also be listening for information that you don't already know.

Creativity, my second operating tool, is a litte more abstract. But to bring it down to earth: you've always got to be looking out for new techniques, new ways to confront your adversaries and to win public understanding and respect. It's not enough to rely on the old techniques of press relations – putting out a news release, for example, or responding when a reporter calls. Traditional press relations are still important, but new challenges will demand new responses and new initiatives. And in many cases, it will be up to you to determine what these will be.

The ability to manage confrontation in a creative way is a major component of leadership, even if it's not the whole story. But you must understand that a commitment to creativity goes against much of the conventional wisdom about management.

Take one of the great American myths – that the successful executive works sixteen hours a day, seven days a week, driving himself (or herself) to the limit all the time. He or she lives in a flurry of activity, rushing out of the board meeting to fly off and review the performance of a subsidiary at the other end of the world, and then rushing back for more meetings. To these people, home and family invariably take a back seat. Perhaps you know people like this. I certainly do, and, to a certain extent, I admire their energy. But I don't necessarily admire their results.

This kind of hectic schedule is rarely the path to creativity. Even if our workaholic 'Type A' CEO is doing a usesful job for his company all sixteen hours a day (which I doubt), there's still no chance to be creative. Creativity doesn't come from hustling 100 per cent of the time. More often, it results from sitting back reflecting. 'Now what if . . . ?'

Years ago, I noticed that I occasionally sit at my desk, staring off into space. Because my office door is usually open, members of my staff sometimes stick their heads in and ask: 'Can I come in? Am I interrupting anything?'

'Come in, by all means,' I'll say. 'But as a matter of fact, yes, you *are* interrupting something.'

What they're interrupting is my fantasizing. Like most people, I occasionally have a good idea right out of the blue. But that's not the sort of thing you can count on; it either happens or it doesn't.

Over the years, I've learned that new ideas are like plants: if you provide them with enough water and light, they're much more likely to grow and to flourish. A regular and deliberate period of fantasizing about future projects and reflecting on current ones often leads me to visions of new programmes – or to refinements of current ones. Again, I'm not talking here about wild flashes of insight or creativity. Like wildflowers, these seem to come along at their own pace, and there's little you can do to hurry them along.

I have in mind something less exotic. In order to move from one point to the next, you've got to move your mind in a certain progression. By visualizing and playing out various scenarios, you'll be better equipped to make things happen. Athletes have long known how to harness their powers of visualization, and we've all seen the interview with the pole-vaulter who performed the record-breaking jump in his mind before attempting it in front of all those people. When it comes to using our imagination in a constructive way, it's clear that those of us who spend our lives behind a desk have some catching up to do.

Or consider another aspect of the workaholic-CEO myth – that there's no time in life for 'luxuries' like arts and culture. Don't you believe it! Even in your business hours, you are going to need to make aesthetic judgments. You may be asked for your opinion on which of two covers is preferable for the annual report. Or you may be called upon to approve a new corporate logo – or perhaps a new building. Clearly, you'll be ahead of the game if you've developed an eye for commercial art. Even if you rarely use these skills, you'll be a broader and a more interesting person for having learned them.

But that's only the beginning. These days, corporations routinely sponsor art exhibitions, concerts, or serious television dramas. As a business leader, you may well be asked to speak at a cultural event. Will you be content to read something your PR person has drafted for you? Or will you be able to show yourself as a sophisticated person who knows something about the world of art?

You should also have some awareness of popular culture. This doesn't mean that you should fall for every new fad, or that you should spend your evenings watching MTV. But it's a good idea to have some awareness of the latest trends in television, books, movies, and fashion. I've known corporate executives who have an excellent command of their own industry, but who don't have the faintest idea of what's happening in the rest of society. While these people are often valuable employees, they're too insular to emerge as effective leaders.

It's important to be tuned into the mainstream. Among other benefits, it will make you better equipped to understand how each project that your company undertakes relates to the larger cultural scene. Keeping up with popular culture also increases your accessibility and provides a natural point of entry into other circles. But perhaps most important, the latest trends are inherently important because they so often represent the best line of vision into the future.

For me, there's always been a third part of the workaholic myth – the cluster of beliefs that says that you as the boss are indispensable; that you are the smartest; that because you give the orders, you know all the answers. Yes, a leader has to be tough. And yes, a leader has to make difficult or unpopular decisions and live with their consequences. But if you want to be a creative leader, there's much more to it than that.

For one thing, you have to lead by example. You can't just order creativity from the people who carry out your projects. You must accept that you'll need people who may be smarter than you in some aspects of your business. If you're a real leader, you'll be able to harness their energy in a way that will enhance your entire enterprise. Only an insecure leader is threatened by the presence of bright or talented people.

By the same token, it's not essential that you start with all of the answers. Far from it. You won't lose stature by admitting ignorance. In fact, asking good, penetrating questions may be the most important thing that a leader can do. I realize, of course, that a great many executives never ask questions. Perhaps they feel that asking questions will make them look vulnerable. Or perhaps they want to give people the impression that they already know everything.

But if you don't ask questions, you'll be making important decisions in a vacuum. Even worse, you may be accepting other people's reports and recommendations at face value. You may not like to see yourself as naive, but the manager who is afraid of asking questions can rarely reach a high level of sophistication.

How do you know what questions to ask? First, you have to overcome your fear of asking the wrong ones. You will, occasionally, ask a stupid question; it's inevitable. But while this may lead to a momentary embarrassment, you will have learned something important that you should have known all along. Better to learn it now rather than later – or not at all.

Another good rule about questions is to put yourself in the other guy's position. In this situation, what would your competitor be asking? Or a consumer? What would a legislator want to know? Or a reporter?

Beyond that, you will want to ask questions of anyone who presumes to give you advice. I often find myself in situations in which somebody tells me that I 'must' take a certain course of action. Whenever I hear that word, I always ask: 'And what happens if I don't?'

Finally, in all you do, you must remain an optimist. Leaders who consistently complain about a bad situation can rarely motivate their troops in a time of crisis. Don't be overly concerned about protecting your rear. Basically, there are two kinds of leaders: the 'let's-nots' and 'why-nots.' Dare to be a why-not leader. Be open to bold and fresh possibilities. If the old answers don't work in new situations, be ready to experiment with new and unconventional solutions.

But enough preaching. In the next chapter, I'll tell you who I am and what I've learned over the past few decades. And then we'll take a detailed look at creative confrontation, and at some of the more important publics that you'll be dealing with in the years ahead.

TWO

Why Am I Telling You These Things?

I HEAR THE QUESTION about once a week, and sometimes, at a meeting or a cocktail party, I can spot it coming: 'Herb, I know you're with Mobil, but what is it, exactly, that you *do*?' Often my questioner is aware that I have some connection with *Masterpiece Theatre*, or with Mobil's op-ed ads in major newspapers, or with one of the many projects that fall under the rubric of my official title, which is Vice-President, Public Affairs. But because that title is so vague, I'm continually being asked questions like 'How do you actually spend your time?' Or, more to the point, 'What's your job over there?'

Until recently, I didn't have a good, snappy answer to these questions. My position carries a number of different responsibilities, but I have always lacked the right phrase that would tie them all together. The only alternative has been to spell out some of my assorted duties.

So, for example, sometimes I describe myself as a lobbyist who tries to raise certain issues and arguments before the public, the government, and the press. But I am also a publisher – of books, pamphlets, reports, and issue-oriented advertisements. In addition, I am a patron of the arts and culture. I am also a corporate spokesman who explains and defends Mobil's point of view. From time to time, I am an advocate who confronts individuals and institutions whose positions are, in our view, wrong or misinformed. And I am a media critic who refuses to allow inaccurate or damaging stories to go unanswered.

In addition to all of this, I am responsible for administering a large department and a hefty budget. As a member of Mobil's board of directors, I participate in corporate investment decisions and other policy issues. When evening rolls around, I often represent the corporation at an art or cultural event, or at a political dinner, or as a guest on a TV interview show.

That just about covers it, but the list is clearly too long to serve as an appropriate answer to those continuing inquiries about my work. After all, I certainly don't want to resemble those poor souls who, when you ask them 'How are you?' actually have the nerve to tell you – and in great detail!

Fortunately, two or three years ago I suddenly realized what all of my various responsibilities added up to: I am, in effect, the manager of an ongoing political campaign. While I don't want to push this analogy too far, there's no question that my job is a lot closer to the confrontational style of politics than it is to the conventional niceties of corporate public relations.

Like any other campaign manager, I'm responsible for a fair amount of research, speech writing, political advertising, and the presentation of issues. I also do my share of fund-raising to support the campaign, although in my case this is accomplished through a rigorous annual budget review rather than the standard dreary cycle of dinners and cocktail parties.

In most respects, the campaign that I work on is similar to conventional political campaigns. But there's also one important difference. Whereas most campaigns are part of the politics of elections, ours belongs to the politics of policy. The chief distinction between the two, of course, is that while the politics of elections is governed by the calendar and has a distinct beginning, middle, and end, the politics of policy is ongoing. From time to time there may be primaries or even decisions on individual issues, but the overall process is never-ending. As a result, we're constantly out there trying to win more votes for our positions.

Now, I'm well aware that the image of an ongoing political campaign is not what most people think of when they hear the phrase 'public relations.' But then this book, as I've said, is not about public relations in the conventional sense.

A friend of mine in Hollywood once distinguished between what he called daytime PR and night-time PR. Night-time PR, he explained, involves securing the tickets to the celebrity events, delivering the flowers to the hotel room, making sure the cars are at the airport, and having the client pose for the right pictures.

Daytime public relations, by contrast, includes such responsibilities as dealing with politicians and political issues, managing confrontations with your opponents, and conceiving creative projects and carrying them through. By now it should be obvious that this book is about daytime public relations.

Before I go any further, I'd like to tell you a little about my background, which has everything to do with the way I operate. Because, believe me, heading up the public-affairs department for a major oil company was just about the last thing I expected to do with my life.

After college (Union, in Schenectady, New York), law school (Columbia), and two years in the Army (intelligence work in Washington), I decided to become a labour lawyer. My first job was with the American Arbitration Association, but after JFK's election to the presidency, which I had worked toward, Robert Kennedy arranged for me to be appointed general counsel to the Federal Mediation and Conciliation Service. Before I came to Mobil, I also worked as a private labour arbitrator and as a professor of labour law. At the same time, I served as a volunteer in a number of election campaigns on the local, state, and national levels.

I arrived at Mobil in 1966, as manager of corporate labour relations. But while I knew a few things about labour unions and political campaigns, I had absolutely no corporate experience. In other words, I ended up in a position for which I had no formal training.

On the other hand, this gap in my education may have been a real advantage. With no corporate training to draw upon, I had to make use of my legal and political background. While I'm proud of my accomplishments, I certainly did not invent the techniques I am best known for, such as creative confrontation, issue advertising in newspapers and magazines, and fighting back against unfairness by the government or the press. I merely brought these skills with me when I moved over from the world of Washington to the world of business.

Until recently, the public relations of politics and of business have always operated by very different sets of values. Political PR has traditionally been aggressive, combative, and confrontational. Business PR, on the other hand, has traditionally been passive, obsequious, and terrified of confrontation. But as politics and business have rubbed up against each other with increasing frequency in recent years, I've had some success in applying the lessons of one to some of the problems of the other.

People say that your education doesn't really begin until you leave school and start working in the real world. I'd have to agree. Whatever I know I've learned by doing, and much of what I learned in those days I still draw upon.

Take negotiating, for example, which is at the heart of both business and politics. As a labour mediator, I soon learned that I couldn't simply walk into a room and impose a settlement on other people. The only way I could succeed was to search constantly for areas of agreement that both sides could live with.

In situations where I myself was a party to the conflict, I saw that I constantly had to imagine myself in the other guy's position. In order to reach an agreement, I had to know what he needed to walk away with. This is all very elementary, of course, but I mention it because I'm continually amazed by how often people in the business world who really should know better fail to understand and act on this fundamental point.

Another lesson I learned from being an arbitrator was the importance of clearly articulating my position. In situations where I couldn't or wouldn't specify exactly what I wanted, I would rarely achieve my goal. In presenting my case, I learned to be wary of generalizations and to be as explicit and as straightforward as possible. And I learned from experience that the best discipline of all is the ability to frame your arguments cogently in writing.

I also learned about the importance of alliances. No matter what kind of situations you're in, it pays to keep an eye out for other individuals and groups whose interests and problems are similar to yours. By the same token, you should always treat your adversaries as potential partners. Today you disagree, but tomorrow, on another issue, you may have to stand together. When the negotiations are over, even if your basic differences remain, you may be required to continue dealing with the people on the other side of the table. They don't disappear simply because you've reached a settlement.

I learned a few other important lessons during this period, and I will be returning to them during the course of this book – like the need to check and recheck all your facts before you state a position, take out an ad, or engage in a debate. During labour negotiations, I would immediately see the consequences whenever one of the participants didn't have his facts straight. More often than not, even a small error would undermine his arguments and his effectiveness.

Another lesson I learned as a mediator was a real respect for the intelligence of 'common' people. In my experience, people usually know what's in their best interest, and they can generally tell when somebody is misleading them. My liberal friends pay lip service to this ideal, but I find that they usually don't believe in the wisdom of letting people make their own decisions. They tend to regard citizens as though they were children, which is one reason that they favour big government and insist on seeing it as a protective nanny.

In my view, that approach is inappropriate and patronizing. I've seen too many 'unskilled' labourers who were as adept as any lawyer in arguing the complexities of the law, or in negotiating settlements. And I've seen too many union members repudiate their leadership when they sensed that their own arguments and interests were not being properly represented to management.

Politics is the other main influence on my life, and my involvement in that world began when I was a child. We lived in New Rochelle, New York, where my father, a small businessman, was active in Democratic politics. In 1936 he ran for State Assembly in our heavily Republican district. Although he lost, we took some consolation in the fact that he ran ahead of his fellow Democrats – including Herbert Lehman, the candidate for governor, and Franklin Roosevelt, who was then seeking his second term as president.

In one of my most vivid childhood memories, I am eight years old, standing outside the Roosevelt School on North Avenue in New Rochelle. It is a bitter November morning, Election Day, 1938, and I am handing out 'palm cards' for the Democratic slate to the people going in to vote. (A palm card was a small replica of the ballot, with one difference: it included only the candidates of one party. Because it was illegal to bring campaign material into the polling place, the card was small enough to fit into your palm.) Later, as an adult, I have continued to be active in political campaigns, ranging from small local elections to presidential races in which I have served as both media adviser and advance man.

In 1960 I worked for John Kennedy, organizing voters in New York. In 1968 I took a leave of absence from Mobil to work on Robert Kennedy's campaign. Eleven years later I took another leave, this time to work as a media adviser for Edward Kennedy in his campaign for the Democratic nomination.

Some of my political experience was as an advance man, which may be the best training you can get for operating in the real world. Before the Secret Service and the other security agencies took the spontaneity out of political campaigns, the advance man did everything. You would go into a city two or three days before the candidate, and you'd be responsible for dozens of details: lining up the right number of hotel rooms, arranging interviews with the local press, planning for police protection, selecting the sites where the candidate should appear, figuring out how to transport people to those sights, how to supply them with flags, and so on. It was trial by fire: you were thrown into a situation where you had no choice but to produce.

I remember going into Kansas City in 1968 just two days before Robert Kennedy announced for the presidency. The candidate was scheduled to fly to Kansas City right after the announcement, and it was up to me to make sure the trip was a political success. I flew into town, checked into a motel, and started making phone calls. I had exactly two days to set up a huge rally at the Kansas City airport, and somehow I pulled it off.

A couple of weeks later, my job was to arrange a whistle-stop campaign train through Oregon. Have you ever tried to line up a train with an observation car? In just a few weeks of a presidential campaign, I gained years of experience. And I learned that the key to a successful project is seeing to it that every detail is performed as well as possible.

In addition to my background in labour law and in politics, there is one other important influence on how I approach my work. I am a serious believer in our system of government, and I hold a particular view of the nature and function of free institutions.

To put it simply, I've never gone along with the common notion that there is a fundamental difference between the individuals and institutions. Institutions, after all, are nothing more than aggregates of people who join together for a common purpose. Legally, in fact, a corporation is a person – an artificial person, to be sure, but a person nonetheless.

Whenever a corporation comes into being, it becomes a corporate person, part of the corporate population, with certain rights, duties, obligations, and immunities. Like human beings, corporations can hold property. They can be sued. And they can also express their views. In fact, in the historic *Bellotti* decision of 1978, the U.S. Supreme Court struck down a Massachusetts law forbidding corporations from spending money to comment publicly on a referendum.

Still, most people continue to cling to the quaint and old-fashioned idea that institutions are – or should be – silent and invisible. There's still a widespread belief that private institutions should be nonpartisan, or worse, that they shouldn't even be interested in public affairs. I don't know about you, but that's not the kind of environment that I want to live in. As far as I'm concerned, our society will remain strong and free only with the support of an aware and active citizenry. And this holds true for institutions as well as individuals.

Most of us take the rights and privileges of our institutions so much for granted that we don't always appreciate that we live in an unusually free and pluralistic society. And we tend to forget that our free institutions don't exist by divine right. Whether we're talking about a steel company or an art museum, every institution has to justify its existence – and not only by providing goods and services.

Now how does a person – or a corporate person – justify his (or its) existence? In a democracy like ours, individuals do it by voting. No matter which candidate they favour, the very act of voting is a gesture of support for the system that makes free elections possible.

Obviously, institutions cannot vote. So what is the commensurate responsibility of free institutions? That's easy – to support other free institutions.

Free institutions are the bedrock of our society. We take them pretty much for granted in America, but from the evidence of other societies in the world, maybe we shouldn't. It's fairly clear that if you restrict the freedom of any one institution – whether it's the press, the labour unions, the church, academia, or the courts – the others will inevitably begin to wither and die. If any of these institutions lose their freedom, the entire society is endangered. In order to function as free people, we need them all.

It follows, then, that those of us whose institutions are economically or politically strong have an obligation to support our fellow institutions whose health may be somewhat more precarious. While I am a frequent critic of the press, for example, my criticisms of newspapers and news broadcasts are directed at strengthening and improving the news media. My worry is that if all of the current abuses continue, the public will eventually begin to demand certain restrictions that could ultimately endanger the freedom of the press.

In addition to helping one another survive, I believe that free institutions and the people who comprise them have a second obligation: to speak out and state their views on the issues of the day. There are those who disagree, of course. They insist that business, religious, and all other types of institutions – as well as the people who lead them – have no right to express their views on political or social topics.

Nonsense! Every person and every institution in our society with something to say should be out there presenting those views to the electorate. Only if the entire spectrum of ideas is made available will the public be able to make an intelligent and rational judgment. Americans have a powerful intuitive ability to understand what's needed and what has to be done.

When I refer to the full range of ideas, I'm not talking about extremists on the radical fringes. While I support their free speech, I'm far more concerned about unpopular views that occasionally emanate from fairly mainstream institutions. Many people don't believe this ever happens; they're under the false impression that the wealthier the organization, the more seriously its views are taken. I wish that were true! If anybody still believes that old canard, I invite them to spend a month working for a major oil company during the next fuel shortage.

The third and final responsibility of free institutions is very simple: to show their face. Just like human persons, corporate persons have distinct personalities. The public-relations function is to present the organization's personality and its philosophy to the various publics that make up the electorate in the ongoing political campaign.

If you're under the impression that corporations don't have personalities, it may be because so many have tried so hard to hide theirs. Many corporations are shy, timid, or even depressed. And a few are actually schizophrenic or otherwise disturbed, and could benefit from some professional help.

Many other corporations, however, have a clear and positive sense of self. Take IBM, for example, which is generally perceived as one of the best managed and most technologically advanced companies in the world. Its products excite people, and the company is always on the cutting edge of change. Its management apparently cares about the health of the larger society, and IBM shows that care through its sponsorship of cultural events. Moreover, IBM's advertising is always well designed, and the company has made a clear commitment to visual quality in all of its operations.

Coca-Cola is another successful company, but one with a very different image. Coke is the Chevrolet of soft drinks. If IBM conjures up an image of white shorts and boardrooms, Coke makes you think of baseball and a hot dog. This is the quintessential America, loved at home and often hated abroad.

Of course, it's not only corporations that have personalities; whole industries do, too. The public's perception of the oil industry's personality and image is an interesting case in point. Indeed, if you consciously set out to choose an industry whose public image had all of the ingredients of the perfect villain, Big Oil would be the ideal choice.

To begin with, crude oil is an essentially dirty product. Second, from the consumer's point of view, buying petrol for the car is not always convenient. Third, the major companies in our industry are extremely large, which by itself leads to hostility from the public. In addition, we do business with foreign nations that are not always popular in this country.

To make matters worse, there is considerable confusion as to our real identity. In the mind of the public, we are often confused with the Texas oil entrepreneurs, the world of *Dallas*. In actual fact, there's very little connection between Big Oil and the Texas entrepreneurs. They have vast wealth and own their own companies. Their operations are almost entirely concentrated in the southwestern states, and they reflect the parochial values of that region. The officers of large oil companies, on the other hand, are simply hired managers who run publicly owned companies. But as far as most people are concerned, oil is oil.

In case all of these problems weren't enough to deal with, our industry has experienced two major international crises during the past twelve years. And despite a total lack of supporting evidence, the public has found it easy and convenient to conclude that the large oil companies are so big, so powerful, and so rich that fuel shortages and price increases must be the result of their conspiratorial manipulations, rather than the fluctuations of a free market.

To put it mildly, all of these concerns have made for quite a challenge. Conventional public relations has generally been concerned with how to get people to see you in mythical terms, rather than how you really are. Our problem is the reverse: we want to help people see past the myths so they can understand who we really are and how we operate. That's why we require a visible and articulate presence, not only in the economic marketplace, but also in the marketplace of politics and ideas.

This, then, is my background and my perspective. It's only fair that you should know these things about me so you can evaluate my positions in view of my particular view of the world. By now, it should be obvious that I don't shy away from offering my opinions, and that these opinions tend to reflect the interests of business executives in medium and large corporations who must deal with the public – whether or not their titles happen to include the words 'public relations.'

Throughout this book, I have drawn upon my own experiences as well as the collective corporate experiences of my employer, Mobil Oil. In today's complex corporate society, no single individual can achieve much of anything on his own, and the projects I will be describing have all depended upon the support and the talents of both my colleagues and top management. If I concentrate only on projects in which I have personally been involved, it's simply because I prefer to discuss the things I know best.

THREE

The Art of Creative Confrontation

IF THE VERY IDEA OF confrontation makes you nervous, at least you're not alone. Most people, even in the highest levels of corporate America, generally prefer to avoid confrontation at any cost. Their attitude reminds me of one of my favourite Jewish jokes: Two Jews in czarist Russia are arrested on a false charge of treason. After a mock trial, they are quickly sentenced to death. The next morning, as the convicted men are being marched to the firing squad, one of them calls out: 'I'd like a final cigarette.'

'Shut your mouth,' says his friend. 'Don't make trouble!'

I used to think that those who shied away from confrontation were somehow opposed to it on principle. But over the years, I've come to understand that most people actually enjoy a confrontation – so long as it is engaged in by other people, or other institutions. In other words, confrontation is most appealing as a spectator sport. These same men and women who are fascinated by a good confrontation are usually reluctant to engage in one themselves.

Where does this hesitation come from? Many people are simply afraid of confrontation, and would love to engage in it if only they had the nerve. Others assume that confrontation is necessarily unpleasant, or that it is extremely difficult. Finally, and perhaps most important, confrontation is seen in some circles as lying outside of the rules of the game. In other words, it's something that gentlemen and ladies just don't do.

During the course of my career, I've seen many intelligent and competent managers fail to solve obvious problems simply because they've refused to confront them directly. In most cases, these people can analyse the problem intellectually, and can even come up with an effective solution. But when that solution requires direct and personal involvement in a confrontational situation, they'll go to great lengths to avoid it. More often than not, this kind of passive response leads either to bad decision making or – just as bad – no decision making.

Sometimes an executive is afraid of confronting a particular individual – an unrealistic boss, for example, or an incompetent employee. Or perhaps the potential confrontation may have to do with a policy issue or a particular business problem. But whatever kind of confrontatiuon is being avoided, the avoiders usually rationalize their behaviour – or lack of behaviour – by believing that if they ignore the problem, it will go away.

Unfortunately, that rarely happens. With few exceptions, a problem that you ignore is a problem that will fester. Count on it: it will return to haunt you. The body of an institution has something in common with the body of a person – if there's something organically wrong, and you ignore it, the problem will only get worse. In business, as in medicine, the sooner you act to confront a difficult situation, the greater your chances of success.

The guiding principle of this book is that confrontation is good for you. I should make clear that by 'confrontation' I'm not talking here about a swaggering or macho pose. Nor does confrontation have to be rude or abusive. But the willingness to engage in good, clean imaginative confrontation – when it is called for – is just about the best tool you can have at your disposal.

If you engage in confrontation when the situation calls for it, you'll not only feel better, but you'll also be more effective in your job. If you develop a reputation for dealing with problems directly, when they first come up, you will soon come to be regarded as a leader who gets the job done.

As you'll see in a moment, there are situations that are immediate threats to you, and in which you'll have no alternative but to respond. Later in this chapter, I'll examine situations in which the threat is considerably more subtle and, for that very reason, more pernicious. In these cases, confronting the problem may appear to be a discretionary response.

Confrontation is psychologically difficult at first, but it's uniquely effective. You may also find that it will generate a fair amount of favourable attention in the press – which brings me back to the popularity of confrontation as a spectator sport. Everybody loves to see a good fight, and this is especially true of the news media.

Before I tell you about some of the confrontations I've been involved in at Mobil over the years, let me outline several general principles that have been helpful to me.

• *Grab the good words – and the good concepts – for yourself.* Or, to put it more elegantly, be sensitive to semantic infiltration, the process whereby language does the dirty work of politics. As you may have noticed, virtually every issue evokes words and phrases that have strong emotional connotations. Be sensitive to these word choices, and be competitive in how you use them. Your objective is to wrap yourself in the good phrases while sticking your opponents with the bad ones.

Unfortunately, I learned this the hard way. The self-described 'public-interest' crowd – and that very phrase is an example of what I'm talking about – has been brilliant at sticking business and industry with the bad words. Remember the 'windfall-profits' tax? Or, for that matter, 'obscene profits'? There was no opportunity for real debate on that topic, for once these phrases were introduced into the discussion, the oil industry had already lost.

Other examples come readily to mind. 'Big business' is a loaded term, because 'big' has come to be identified with 'bad.' In the ongoing debate over tax reform, the business community refers to lower corporate taxes as 'incentives,' while antibusiness forces speak of 'tax breaks.' On the international scene, whether guerrillas are seen as 'terrorists' or 'freedom fighters' depends on what side you're on. The communist world has been grabbing the good words for years: consider The People's Republic of China, a brilliant name for a totalitarian regime.

Similarly, you should try to identify yourself with good concepts – especially those that your opponent thinks he has locked up. During the national debate on the energy crisis, the popular liberal view was that conservation alone would save us, and that we all had to cut back on our standard of living. We at Mobil disagreed, and we infuriated our opponents by making our case in anti-elitist terms: 'You and I may be well off,' we argued, 'but one-third of this nation is still poor. Their only hope lies in continued growth. Are you willing to go down to Watts or up to Harlem and tell the people living there to cut back on their expectations?'

• *Don't be predictable.* In your dealings with competitors and opponents, try not to be predictable. This will add to your power, as other people will spend time trying to figure out what you're likely to do. Remember that in a football game, the defensive team has a lot more problems if the opponent's offence is capable of a few surprises. They key word here is *capable*. You don't have to be surprising in every encounter, but the mere awareness that you might do something unexpected can be very helpful to your side.

• *In a debate, go first.* This rule goes against all of the conventional wisdom – which should make it easier to put into practice. But debates have something in common with chess, where whoever plays the white pieces makes the first move. During the opening of a chess game, black is invariably forced to respond to white's opening moves. White's advantage is thought to be so significant that in a chess match, the players alternate playing the white pieces. A debate – and I mean that word in its largest sense – presents a similar opportunity. Whoever leads off sets the agenda, while the other person is forced to react at least in part. So whenever you're involved in a confrontation, try to set the agenda by getting your side of the story out first.

• *Show your thought process – not just your conclusions.* Never assume that your opponents or the spectators necessarily share your basic assumptions. If you merely state your conclusions without providing any indication of how you reached them, you're not going to convince anyone. But if you can explain how and why you arrived at those conclusions, it may be possible to change a few minds.

Always be willing to lead your opponents and your audience through your thought process. Outline the facts that you find so compelling. Reveal the underpinnings of your philosophy. Show, in rational steps, how you arrived at the conclusions that you now find so obvious. By disclosing your thought process, you're treating your audience with respect instead of talking down to them. And you'll also be doing yourself a favour, because a constant reexamination of your arguments will sharpen your position and expose any flaws in your thinking.

• *Know when you've lost.* Not every confrontation will be successful, and there's nothing sadder that watching good people squander their time, energy, and personal prestige on a losing situation. Accept in advance that you won't win every battle, and that your resources are best spent on situations in which you have a fighting chance.

Losing, like winning, should be handled graciously. Was your fight a matter of principle? You can continue to uphold the principle even if you give up the fight. But whenever it's clear that you can't win, cut your losses and move on.

Let's look now at several different types of confrontation.

CONFRONTING DAMAGING RUMOURS

Back in 1973, I had to confront a series of rumours that swept the country while causing immeasurable damage to our company and our industry. In retrospect, we should have dealt with these rumours more quickly and more forcefully than we did. While we did act, we didn't act boldly enough. And it's a mistake we're still paying for.

The rumours seem to have begun in New York. Early in December of 1973, several months into the Arab oil embargo and the subsequent energy crisis, a man in Montauk, Long Island, called the *New York Times* to report what he believed was an unusual number of oil tankers offshore. Around the same time, a Staten Island man called the *Newark Star-Ledger* to say that he had seen some tankers in New York's lower harbour. The implication in both of these reports was that the tankers, which belonged to the major oil companies, were waiting for oil prices to rise before discharging their cargoes.

Both newspapers checked the report with the port captain and the Coast Guard. They were informed that the flow of tankers was normal for that time of the year, and that in view of the gasoline shortage, there were, if anything, too few ships. With no corroborating evidence, there was, of course, no story.

But the rumours continued. All through December, newspapers, wire services, and radio and TV news desks took calls from people who insisted that they had seen or heard of 'fleets of oil tankers' standing in harbours or lurking offshore. The Coast Guard continued checking these reports. As the stories mushroomed, the Coast Guard began to compare radioed notices of expected ship entries with actual arrivals twenty-four hours later. They found no significant increase in traffic, and no hold-up of the regular flow of oil.

When the media came calling, those of us in the public-relations departments of the major oil companies flatly denied the rumours. Not only were the stories ridiculous, we explained, but they rested on a faulty premise. There was, in fact, nothing to be gained by delaying unloading of the oil. Under the price-control laws, shippers were limited to a sale price based on what they had paid initially for the oil. In other words, the American price of oil had been established from the moment the ship was loaded.

Besides, we added, it was very expensive to keep a tanker at sea.

If there was any economic motivation at work, it would have been to speed up the deliveries. There was certainly no point in delaying them.

Just as the story appeared to be dying in New York, it cropped up in Chesapeake Bay. And in Philadelphia. And Baltimore. And then in Florida and in Texas and around the Great Lakes. 'Thousands' of barges were said to be jamming the Mississippi and Ohio Rivers – all waiting for prices to go up.

In some cases, it turned out, there were a number of barges on those rivers. But they were carrying grain and ore, not oil. When it came to oil barges, the traffic was normal.

Then, during Christmas week, an airline pilot reported seeing a group of tankers clustered five hundred miles southeast of New York. Because there was no corroboration, the report was not used in print or on the air. But it quickly spread by word of mouth.

Finally, on December 29, the *New York Times* ran a front-page article that gave some credence to the rumours. According to David Andelman, who wrote it, the story was published because the reports finally had an 'authoritative source.' The day before the story ran, Brendan T. Byrne, governor-elect of New Jersey, had attended an editorial lunch at the *Times*, at which he charged that 'the tankers were out there waiting for their price.'

By now the rumours were completely out of control. On January 3, William E. Simon, administrator of the Federal Energy Office, issued a strong statement on the subject of the mythical tankers: 'Such reports are unfounded in fact and do not reflect an accurate understanding of petroleum pricing regulations,' he said. Simon cited federal reports that tanker movements were 'normal and in accordance with the usual patterns observed in the past.'

In retrospect, we ought to have protested when the *Times* failed to give Mr Simon's denial the same page-one prominence it had given the rumours a week earlier. The denial, of course, wasn't as exciting as the rumours, so it was printed on page 13.

By this time, reports of the tankers were commonplace on radio and television. Among those who perpetuated the story was Geraldo Rivera of ABC's local New York affiliate, although, to be fair, Rivera also took the trouble to interview Senator Jacob Javits. 'We can't kid ourselves by laying the energy crisis at the door of the oil companies,' Javits told him, adding that 'the fact that you hadn't seen all those tankers before is just the fact that you hadn't been out in the harbour before.'

As late as the last week of March, the *Newark Star-Ledger* received a call from a New Jersey coastal resident. Apparently there was a whole fleet of tankers offshore . . .

How did we at Mobil respond to this unusual crisis? At first, we took routine measures. We issued periodic statements to the press denying the rumours. We also distributed William Simon's statement, together with our own, to all of our shareholders, employees, dealers, distributors, and major customers.

But this wasn't enough, and we knew it. The problem we were facing was, at least in our experience, unprecedented. First, there *were* tankers out there – the same ships that were always there, when nobody was interested. Second, the country was gripped by hysteria, with a large segment of the public convinced that the oil companies were engaged in a conspiracy. Third, both the Congress (for political reasons) and the public (for emotional reasons) required a scapegoat to explain how the United States could be held hostage by the Arab states. Fourth, there was – or so it seemed – official corroboration of the tanker rumours from major political figures who were eager to jump on the anti-oil company bandwagon. Finally, it was virtually impossible to disprove the rumours – for how could we convincingly show the *absence* of tankers?

We needed an independent way to trace the history of the rumours. Where did the story begin, and how did it come to be so widely believed? The answer to these questions would have made for a fascinating article in almost any newspaper or magazine. But given the atmosphere at that time, this wasn't a story we ever expected to read.

We had no choice but to commission the story ourselves. We found a reputable free-lance investigative reporter and gave him free rein to track down the reports and to determine for himself whether they were true. Peter Celliers's article, which traced the history of the tanker rumours and exonerated the oil industry, was eventually published in *The Bulletin* of the American Society of Newspaper Editors. We at Mobil reprinted the article, and I have drawn upon it here to tell this story.

Naturally, it would have been far better for our side if a prominent journalist like Tom Wicker or Jack Anderson had written a column on the tanker hoax. But no big-name reporter was interested in the story, and because Peter Celliers was not widely known, the impact of his article was limited.

What else could we have done? With hindsight, of course, the answers come more easily. To start with, we should have challenged our critics to a debate. We should have offered to pay a million dollars to anyone who could prove that the rumours were true. Better yet, we should have hired a large helicopter and invited a group of prominent politicians and press people to fly anywhere they wanted and to show us all of these tankers. We should have said to our critics: 'If you really believe there are tankers out there, show us where. We'll even help you look for them!'

Looking back, it's clear that we failed to confront this situation directly. It was a mistake and a failure on our part, and the spectre of this episode still haunts me.

What prevented us from taking effective action to deal with the myth of the tankers? In retrospect I suspect it's that the story was so ludicrous to those of us in the oil industry that we didn't fully understand how seriously it was being taken by the public – until it was too late. At one point, I remember, I was so frustrated that I started telling reporters, off the record, that there really were tankers lurking out there, but that they weren't really carrying any oil. Instead, they were loaded with *money*. With a straight face, I explained that we were making so much money from the oil crisis that the banks had no more room to store it all! Fortunately, nobody took me seriously, but in that atmosphere, I now realize, it was just possible that somebody might have.

What are the lessons to be learned from this episode? First, no matter how much experience you have and how much you prepare for emergencies, there will always be problems that you can't anticipate – and that you can't completely solve.

Second, when you're dealing with errors and distortions, you have to correct them as quickly and as publicly as you can. By the time we made our response, it was too little and too late. Had I known then what I know now about the need to confront the emergence of rumours quickly, directly, and forcefully, I would have acted more boldly.

Third, you can't always respond to an irrational event in a rational way. You have to be as dramatic in your response as the irrationality of the rumours demand. You've got to get in front of the rumour, rather than trailing behind it. When you've got a fire raging out of control, pouring water on it isn't always enough. Sometimes you have to fight fire with fire.

Even so, you won't always be successful. To this day, there are still millions of Americans who believe that those tankers were really out there. But even with hindsight, I'm not sure how we could have defeated that appealing fantasy. As Mark Twain once said, 'A lie gets halfway around the world before truth puts on its boots.'

CONFRONTING TELEVISION NEWS SHOWS

According to the polls, something like 75 per cent of the public say that television is their main source of information. Moreover, because television is so emotional in its effect, the message it conveys is often more important than the information that viewers receive from other sources.

Unfortunately, as we'll soon see, even when that information is wrong, the lords of television have made it very difficult to confront television *on* television. So if you want to confront television news, for example, you're at an enormous disadvantage. While there are some ways to confront television, it's important to understand that there are limitations on what these techniques will achieve. In most cases, you will have little chance of correcting inaccuracies and distortions. On the other hand, it may be possible to prevent such problems from occurring in the future.

My concern is not only that television presents greater problems than the print media. I could tolerate that, if only television were willing to build in the safeguards that the print media take for granted. Over the years, we at Mobil, together with many other organizations, have taken advantage of the various mechanisms that newspapers and magazines have developed to correct some of their own shortcomings.

First, most major American newspapers have instituted an op-ed page specifically designed to encourage various and diverse points of view on major issues. Second, a growing number of newspapers have hired an ombudsman, a kind of in-house referee who has the power to challenge the inevitable examples of bias and distortion that are endemic to all media. Third, virtually all newspapers and magazines (with the curious exception of *The New Yorker*) publish letters to the editor, in which any individual or organization can correct errors of fact or opinion, offer a viewpoint, or seek redress for unfair treatment. Fourth, newspapers and magazines have a long tradition of accepting advertising not only for goods and services, but also for a discussion of major issues.

Television is different, and television news has its own distinct set of limitations. To start with, in the mere half hour that is devoted to national news on the commercial networks, there is never enough time to cover any issue in depth. At the height of the energy crisis, for example, the *New York Times* often devoted several full pages solely to energy reporting. Television news, by contrast, could rarely give the story more than four or five minutes.

In addition, the journalists who work for the network news shows tend to be journalists. In most cases, they lack the training to cover a complex or technical economic story. During the energy crisis, stories were breaking so quickly that reporters with very little knowledge about energy were often drafted from other beats to become instant 'energy experts.' Moreover, network television news does not use free-lance journalists. All of the reporters are part of the network organization. If somebody from the network didn't see the event, it didn't take place.

Perhaps most important, the network news programmes are fundamentally entertainment shows. John J. O'Connor, the television critic of the *New York Times*, put it well when he wrote that 'TV news, no matter how lofty its pronounced aims, is rarely able to escape the clutches of show business considerations.' Like all other entertainment on television, the news shows are planned and executed with at least one eye on the ratings. And if there's one thing to which the ratings do not respond, it's a serious discussion of important public issues. Topics like business economics, which can be critical to the lives of television viewers, are generally seen by TV news executives as too dull or complex to be given more than lip service.

Unlike some of my colleagues, I didn't believe that the network news departments were necessarily biased against the oil companies and big business. But with all of the limitations of TV news, it soon became clear that we would be unlikely to see fair and complete coverage of the energy story – not to mention our perspective on it. While the print media were willing to sell us space and rarely disagreed with us over the substance or the placement of an issue-oriented ad, we soon discovered that the TV networks were very different. They wanted to judge what we could say, and they were prepared to exercise their powers in a way that seemed to us arbitrary.

So before examining several confrontations over the content of television news shows, let's look first at a confrontation over the rules of access.

THE PROBLEM OF ACCESS

In the early 1970s, we at Mobil were becoming increasingly frustrated with the media's coverage of the energy issue. Despite our best efforts to supply information and to make our top executives available for interviews, the energy crisis was all too often portrayed simplistically and wrongly as a conspiracy by the oil companies to take advantage of the public.

To present our side of the story, we decided to respond with a series of commercial messages that would make an argument rather than sell a product. While we were well aware that it's almost impossible to communicate very much of substance in a sixty-second spot, we believed that an imperfect response was better than none.

Unfortunately, our messages proved almost impossible to get on the air. All three networks advised us that their policies precluded the showing of commercials that dealt with issues of public importance. In some cases, even the use of the word 'profit' in our proposed copy was enough to cause a rejection or a request for deletion.

Faced with these obstacles, we decided in 1974 to create a TV commercial that would be an all-time, all-weather, indoor-and-outdoor champion for blandness. We began with a shot showing a beach and the ocean. Then the camera moved out to show only the water. The narration began:

> According to the U.S. Geological Survey, there may be 60 billion barrels of oil or more beneath our continental shelves.
>
> Some people say we should be drilling for that oil and gas. Others say we shouldn't because of the possible environmental risks. We'd like to know what you think.
>
> Write Mobil Poll, Room 647, 150 East 42nd Street, New York, New York 10017.
>
> We'd like to hear from you.

NBC accepted the ad. CBS turned it down in a letter, which read in part: 'We regret that the subject matter of this commercial . . . deals with a controversial issue of public importance and does not fall within our "goods and services" limitation for commercial acceptance.' And ABC rejected the ad with no explanation.

Now even if our ad *was* controversial, what was wrong with that? Neither the Supreme Court nor the FCC had ever ruled that commercials shouldn't be controversial, or that issue advertisements were not suitable for broadcasting on television.

Because we couldn't respond to television *on* television, we did the next-best thing: we responded in the print media. We designed a full-page newspaper ad that reproduced both the visuals and the text of our TV spot. The headline was 'Why do two networks refuse to run this commercial?' But this time, instead of asking the public whether we should be allowed to drill for oil, we asked readers if they thought the ad should have been accepted by all three networks. We received over two thousand replies, and the respondents overwhelmingly favoured our right to express our views on the air.

As we saw it, the refusal of two major networks to sell us airtime for even this bland message represented a serious problem. First, this was a clear violation of our First Amendment rights. Second, we were growing increasingly disturbed about the potential of television to distort important information without any checks and balances.

When we finally sat down with the network executives to discuss the problem, they repeatedly cited the fairness doctrine, the mandate of the Congress that requires owners of broadcast licences 'to encourage and implement the broadcast of all sides of controversial public issues' and to play 'a conscious and positive role in bringing about the balanced presentation of the opposing viewpoints.'

As the networks interpret the fairness doctrine, to allow the airing of controversial messages would force broadcasters, in ABC's inimitable words, to grant airtime 'to every kook who comes down the pike.'

In my view, however, the fairness doctrine, as the networks apply it, is fair only to the networks. They use it to protect themselves, rather than to carry out their obligation to the American public. In reality, only a minority of Americans are accurately represented by the two or three 'mainstream' opinions that are generally explored by network newscasters when they examine an issue. Groups with unpopular or minority views – or even views that run counter to the newscaster's own prejudices – have little opportunity to have their opinions aired except when replying to an editorial.

To be fair, it is certainly possible that if we at Mobil were allowed to buy time to state our views, the fairness doctrine might indeed compel the networks to provide free time for a rebuttal of our position. To cover this eventuality, we offered to pay not only for our own messages, but also for any rebuttal time that the networks might be obliged to provide to our opponents. Moreover, we agreed to let the networks decide when a rebuttal was actually required. We even offered to let the networks select an individual or organization to make the response! As far as we could see, these concessions represented a generous and unprecedented offer.

In January 1980 we submitted another ad to the networks. In the wake of the second energy crisis, there had been a great deal of talk about the huge profits of the oil companies. Some of this talk had been on the network news shows, and much of it had been misinformed. We wanted to set the record straight. We wanted people to know that the main reason for our huge profits was that we were a huge company. We wanted the public to understand a fundamental principle of America's economic system – the difference between profits and profitability. So we prepared an ad that made that point in a slightly unusual way.

In the sixty-second spot, a man dressed in a business suit drove into a Mobil service station. As an attendant filled the gas tank, the man made the following comment:

> Oil company profits make a lot of people angry. Take Mobil and its 1979 profits. They were big. But what does 'big' mean? Mobil made about four cents a gallon on petroleum sales. Of course the pennies add up. Which is why Mobil was able to spend over two and a half billion dollars last year to find and produce oil and gas.
>
> To get profits in perspective, business analysts look at percentages, just as you do when you open a savings account. Over the years, Mobil has earned about the same profit percentage on money invested as the average for all manufacturing industries – and less than for ABC, CBS, and NBC.
>
> So isn't it worth four cents on the gallon for Mobil to gas up your car and heat your home? Think about it.

As we expected, the major networks turned down the commercial, although each of them argued that this refusal had nothing to do with the fact that our commercial dared to mention the networks' own profits. But the commercial did appear on Metromedia stations in New York and Los Angeles, and on the ABC affiliate in Washington, where it ran during the evening news broadcasts. Equally important, from our perspective, was that the whole controversy received a fair amount of coverage in the print media.

Around the same time, we took further action. For several years we had been running a number of high-quality TV specials on the commercial networks. But now we decided that as long as the networks would not accept commercials, we would no longer sponsor these programmes. Instead, we set up the Mobil Showcase Network, an ad hoc group of network-affiliated and independent stations all over the country.

The Mobil Showcase Network has been a great success for us, with one exception. In all the years Mobil Showcase has been in operation, the stations that are actually owned and operated by the networks in New York, Los Angeles, and Chicago – the three biggest markets – have never bid for any of our shows. (Perhaps in retirement I'll have the time to learn whether this doesn't represent illegal restraint of trade. In these markets, we've always signed up independent stations.)

One of the nice benefits of the Mobil Showcase Network is that whenever our programmes are shown, the network offering is pre-empted by ours on all the stations that run our show. We generally choose a time slot where one of the major networks is weak, which makes the local affiliates more eager to go with us. In response, the networks sometimes try to pressure the affiliates not to take our shows.

Thanks to the Mobil Showcase Network, we are able to present our own commercials, uncensored, during prime time, on network-affiliated stations. The commercials appear on a day and time of our choice, immediately before and after (but never during) a high-quality show of our choice. The networks are the losers – intellectually, because they are exposed as censors, and economically, because under this arrangement they lose advertising revenues. The pressure on us, of course, is to come up with dramatic shows that are good enough to tempt the stations to risk pre-empting network shows.

While the TV networks have still not agreed to accept issue advertising, a growing segment of the public believes that its time has come. A 1980 survey by the Opinion Research Corporation found that 85 per cent of the American public think that corporations should be allowed to present their views on controversial issues in TV commercials – a 13-point increase from the already high proportion of Americans who held that position in 1978.

The courts, too, seem to favour it: as mentioned earlier, in the historic *Bellotti* decision of 1978, the US Supreme Court struck down a Massachusetts law forbidding corporations from spending money to comment publicly on a referendum. 'The press,' said the Court, 'does not have a monopoly on either the First Amendment or the ability to enlighten.' And two years later, the high court ruled that utility companies had a constitutional right to include public-policy messages with their bills to consumers.

Even broadcasters favour the airing of issue ads on television. In a 1980 survey of television stations by the Television Bureau of Advertisers, an astounding 89 per cent of the TV stations surveyed said they were willing to accept advocacy advertising. Five years earlier, only half of the stations polled were willing.

Not surprisingly, the independent stations are far less nervous than the network affiliates about presenting these ads. In 1976, for example, two of Metromedia's local stations accepted some of our issue ads on an experimental basis. Did they incur any damage? On the contrary. Metromedia said the results left them 'most pleased.' And one of their officers summed up the experiment by saying that when the commercials presented controversial issues of public importance, 'they were explored in depth in separate programming presented by the stations, at which time opposing views were aired. . . . The Mobil spots thus served as an impetus for discussion of important national problems.'

We are also allowed to air issue viewpoints during intermissions of a music series we sponsor on WQXR, the Manhattan radio station owned by the *New York Times*. Our messages, which are adapted for radio from our op-ed print ads, have triggered no crisis of 'fairness'. This is what the station manager said about our campaign on WQXR: 'It doesn't worry us. This is stimulating programming for our particular audience. If Mobil says something that justifies another point of view being heard, we would make time available. . . . We think this makes the station more lively.'

After all these years, we are still battling the networks on the issue of free access. Time and the public are on our side, and eventually our view will prevail. So far, of course, we have not won the fight. But at this point, it's just a matter of time.

ABC'S OIL DOCUMENTARY

On March 20, 1974, in the midst of the first energy crisis, ABC broadcast a documentary entitled *Oil: The Policy Crisis*. Jules

Bergman, the narrator, stated at the outset that 'this programme is a primer on oil and oil policy. It is designed to help understand the current crisis. If there's confusion in the public mind on the so-called energy crisis today, the problem did not begin yesterday or last October.'

Two days before the documentary aired nationally, the network invited us to comment on the programme. In its telegram, ABC described the show as 'basically a primer on oil, designed to help Americans understand a highly charged and difficult problem.' The network also maintained that the documentary had been 'researched and executed from every conceivable point of view.'

Given this description, we expected a balanced and educational programme. In retrospect, we were shockingly naive. Viewing the show, we found thirty-two separate inaccuracies or examples of unfairness. Moreover, much of the documentary was devoted to events dating back fifty years and more, including historical film clips of John D. Rockefeller, the Teapot Dome, wooden derricks and 'gushers,' all of which was fundamentally irrelevant to the stated purpose of the programme. Many of the clips portrayed an image that was damaging to the industry, leaving the impression that this negative image was equally deserved today.

What was missing from the documentary was no less interesting. There was no mention of the history of government price controls on natural gas. There was no mention of the moratorium on drilling off Santa Barbara since 1969. Nor was there any mention of the surge in the consumption of gasoline that followed the rising use of power options on cars and the imposition of rigorous exhaust emission controls.

During the previous four years, America's demand for imported oil had increased by 130 per cent to nearly eight million barrels a day. As a result, one of the major problems facing this country in 1974 was how to reach a proper balance between our needs for energy and our legitimate environmental objectives. With regard to these key issues, *Oil: The Policy Crisis* had virtually nothing to say.

Finally – and this was really hard to believe – there was only a passing mention of the Arab oil embargo, and no mention at all of the recent cutback in Arab production. These two forces together made for a shortfall in oil of more than two million barrels a day. Was it really possible to discuss the energy crisis without dealing with our dangerous dependence on foreign sources of oil?

In a situation like this, the conventional response is to ask for a meeting with the offending network. You tell those responsible what's wrong with the show, they listen and nod piously, and then they go and make the same mistakes all over again. I had already discovered that this kind of private confrontation is of no real value. Just as ABC went public with its charges, we would go public with ours.

We decided to file a brief with the National News Council, a private watchdog of national news media, asking it to investigate our complaint that ABC's show was inaccurate and shoddily researched. Concurrently, we issued a press release about our complaint, which dealt with some of the specific aspects of the programme that we found objectionable. The controversy received a good amount of coverage in the print media, including the *Wall Street Journal*, which labelled the show 'an hour-long editorial.'

The analysis that we submitted to the National News Council ran twenty-two pages. In the document, we cited the thirty-two unfair or misleading statements from the programme, together with our responses. For example:

QUOTE: Today the petroleum industry is dominated by about 18 integrated companies . . .

RESPONSE: Even if the oil industry were 'dominated' by 18 companies, it still would be one of the least concentrated industries in the country. The oil industry is much less concentrated than autos, steel, computers, and many others. The single largest oil refiner has less than 10 per cent of total US refining capacity. . . . Television broadcasting, on the other hand, has only three 'majors'.

QUOTE: We also know that the nation's distress is extremely profitable to the oil industry.

RESPONSE: Over the past 10 years, Mobil's return on shareholders' equity in the United States averaged 9.3%. By comparison, the average return for all US manufacturing industries was 11.6%. . . . In 1973, Mobil's return on average shareholders' equity in the United States was 10.1% compared with an estimated 12.6% for the average of all manufacturing industries. ABC's return on shareholders' equity for 1973 was about 17%.

While the National News Council did not see fit to investigate our complaints of factual inaccuracies and other distortions, it issued a statement saying that ABC's documentary 'could, and did, select certain facts that pointed in one direction and omit others that pointed elsewhere.' The council also said that the network was guilty of leading viewers to assume that the programme was 'striving conscientiously for balance and fairness. In cultivating that impression,' the council noted, 'ABC was professing adherence to a standard higher than was required of it and higher than it in fact achieved.' The council also expressed the opinion that ABC should not have contended that the documentary was 'executed from every conceivable point of view.'

Although the council's verdict fell far short of our expectations, it included enough language favourable to our position to enable us to put out a press release claiming victory. Which brings up a useful principle: When you're involved in a public dispute, if there's any basis for claiming victory, do so quickly and publicly. The early bird gets the favourable press coverage – which we did in this case.

We also benefitted from a second useful principle that helped us get our point across. Newspaper and magazine journalists are generally eager to expose and criticize their television colleagues at every possible opportunity. So although we did not achieve a full victory, our taking the matter to the National News Council led to so much favourable press coverage that we won the case with the public.

We did not, of course, succeed in correcting the record in the minds of the people who saw the ABC documentary. But short of owning our own network, that was an impossible goal. We did achieve something more modest, but important in its own right: we served ABC notice that if it ever pulled a stunt like that in the future, we would not hesitate to go public with our complaints and embarrass the network professionally. We also showed our employees and our stockholders – not to mention the government – that during this period of extreme pressure, we were willing to fight for what we believed in.

WNBC AND 'THE GREAT GASOLINE WAR'

When WNBC-TV, the New York affiliate of the national network, announced that it would run a series called 'The Great Gasoline War' on its 6:00 pm news show during the week of February 23–27, 1976, we decided to pay close attention. We knew that our suspicions were well founded when the very first episode included that wonderful old story about the oil tankers waiting off the coast until there was a price rise. The subsequent episodes were filled with other distortions and errors. As each episode was aired, we monitored it closely and developed our responses.

Over the weekend, we prepared a full-page newspaper ad headed 'What ever happened to fair play?' which ran in the *New York Times*, the *New York Daily News*, and the eastern edition of the *Wall Street Journal*. In the ad, we described the WNBC programme as 'inaccurate, unfair and a disservice to the people.' We called it 'a parade of warmed-over distortions, half-truths, and downright untruths marching across the screen like an army of tired ghosts – ghosts we thought had been laid to rest years ago.'

But that was only rhetoric; what we needed was substance. And so we outlined and documented seventeen separate 'hatchet jobs,' with a small drawing of a hatchet next to each of the distortions.

We had heard that this same series of reports was going to be repeated by other NBC affiliates around the country. So as soon as the ad was ready, we sent a copy to the station managers of each of these local stations. We'll never know for sure, but it's certainly possible that this mailing had something to do with the fact that no other station in the country aired the series.

While the ad was being prepared, we wrote to WNBC and asked to purchase half an hour of time in order to present additional information that we felt was pertinent to the many issues raised by Liz Trotta, the narrator of the series.

The station refused our request. In a telegram, WNBC invited a company spokesperson to appear live on its news show. (We had already turned down an opportunity to appear on the documentary, because we suspected that the interview would be chopped up and would result in a brief segment that had little to do with the points we wanted to make.) 'Since you fear editing of your statements,' the news director wrote, 'I am offering to allow you to make a short statement followed by questions by Ms Trotta. Please let me know when you can have a spokesperson available.'

At this point, many people would have been inclined to accept the station's offer. After all, from the station's point of view, having our representative appear live on the news was a real concession. And isn't half a loaf better than none?

Not always. 'Why should Liz Trotta be asking *us* questions?' I demanded. 'She's the culprit here. If anything, she should be allowed to make a statement, and then we should ask *her* questions.'

That, at any rate, was our private response. In our press release, we called the station's offer 'patently unfair' because it would be impossible for us to compress our response into a short statement to reply to five nights of one-sided editorializing.

What did we achieve in this confrontation? As with the previous one, we served notice to the news media that if reporting on our company was not accurate, we would not hesitate to go public with our complaints. And again, we showed our supporters and allies that we were willing to fight to present the truth as we saw it.

CBS AND MOBIL'S PROFITS

Several years later, on October 23, 1979, CBS network reporter Ray Brady announced on the *Evening News* that Mobil Oil's 'profit report' was due on the following day, and that 'oil analysts say they expect the company's increase in profits will be spectacular.'

The following morning, in a report on Mobil's 'profit increases,' Bob Schieffer followed up 'spectacular' with 'tremendous.' Later that day, we received several calls from a *CBS Evening News* researcher, who asked us for the news release on Mobil's earnings. We promised to issue the details later that day.

While our messenger was en route to CBS, we called the researcher to offer an oral summary of the more important statistics and the reasons for them. But CBS was not interested in explanations. All the researcher wanted to know were the earnings for the third quarter and for the first nine months of 1979, with the comparable figures for 1978. The network took the figures on our worldwide petroleum earnings per gallon sold, but declined figures describing rates of return.

That night, despite ample time to review our news release and utilize pertinent information on how and where our money was made, CBS chose to place one fact from the release – that our third-quarter earnings were up 131 per cent over the previous year – into a 'hunched' report on how oil companies 'earn a foreign profit from an American consumer.'

In other words, on the hunch that Mobil's earnings would be large, CBS had prepared a story days in advance about the source of those earnings. Although our news release contained information that directly contradicted CBS's thesis, the network proceeded with its guess and Ray Brady aired his story while standing in front of a Mobil petrol station sign.

In the segment, Ray Brady charged that the oil companies engaged in phony book-keeping practices that allowed them to earn a foreign profit from an American consumer. He interviewed Edwin Rothschild, a politically-motivated critic of the oil industry, who charged that the oil companies were spreading some of their American profits to their foreign subsidiaries. Brady then concluded his report with a fantastic scenario in which oil companies sold Mideast crude from one of their subsidiaries to another, with significant price increases on each transaction. With the Mobil sign in the background, Brady's words carried the inference that Mobil was guilty of this scam.

Unfortunately for CBS, our October 24 announcement had gone into great detail as to the sources of our foreign earnings, and had laid out a number of facts that did not fit into the Ray Brady scenario. Besides, Mobil's activities, like those of all of the major oil companies, are regularly and thoroughly audited by the IRS. We have been subjected to countless government investigations. No responsible person has ever suggested the existence of the kind of practices described by Ray Brady.

Brady's remarks had taken the familiar form of 'the oil companies say this, but their critics say that,' leaving viewers with the impression that the truth was somewhere in the middle, or that there was at least a kernel of truth to the charges. He dismissed the industry's case by saying that 'oil companies argue that many of their profits go to shareholders as dividends,' but neglected to mention that an amount in excess of profits is invested in finding and producing new energy supplies.

From our point of view, the Ray Brady segment was the worst and most unfair report on our earnings that we had yet seen. We called CBS and pointed out the errors in the broadcast. We asked to see the full tape of the interview with the British oil analyst who had also appeared on the show. We asked who else had been interviewed for the segment. We asked for airtime to correct the erroneous impressions the broadcast had created. CBS refused all of these requests.

We then made a formal written request for 'sufficient uncensored time on CBS Evening News to correct last night's highly misleading Ray Brady report on Mobil's profits.' Not surprisingly, CBS refused again.

Denied access to the network, we responded with two facing full-page print advertisements that appeared in the major newspapers and in *Time* magazine. Entitled 'How CBS on October 24, 1979, prefabricated the news,' the ad included the entire transcript of the segment, followed by our response. The second ad went on to detail '19 dull and unsensational facts about our profits the TV networks didn't tell you – and won't allow us to tell you.'

From everything we heard, there was a major impact at CBS News. They knew they had handled this one badly. To respond to their critics, they even prepared a two-page form letter, signed by Walter Cronkite himself. As with any confrontation, both sides in the faceoff received a fair amount of media attention.

What did we achieve by these four confrontations with television? First, we went against the conventional wisdom that you can't argue with the press, and that you have to accept all of its abuses without protest. In all of these cases, we made a convincing argument with a great amount of detail. We documented every charge we made. In the cases in which we took out ads to make our case against the television networks, our amassing of documentation was impressive. Those who actually read the ads could see that we had the facts on our side, while those who merely glanced at them might easily have concluded, 'Gee, if they went to all of this trouble and expense, they must have a legitimate complaint.'

A second achievement of these confrontations is that they served notice that we would hit back if we were unfairly attacked. Our protests led to professional embarrassment among those who had distorted the news. It was our hope that the guilty parties would think twice before making the same mistake in the future.

Finally, we showed a variety of other groups, including employees, shareholders, consumers, and the government, that we cared deeply about our reputation, and that we weren't going to allow distortions about us to go unanswered. We strengthened our existing constituency, and perhaps we even changed a few minds.

Instead of complaining, moaning, or whining, we took a more professional and clinical approach. In effect, we said to the public: 'Here's what they say; here's what we say. You decide who's right.' In short, we confronted the networks by treating ourselves as their equals.

CONFRONTING POWERFUL PUBLIC FIGURES

The conventional wisdom is that it's suicidal for a private institution to take on a powerful individual or office. Most people think that if you dare to seek a confrontation with the White House, you'll end up in very hot water – or at least with major tax problems. But the wonderful thing about our country is that any individual or institution can seek to redress a grievance against any other individual or institution, either in a court of law or in the court of public opinion. If the need arises, don't be reluctant to avail yourself of this privilege.

If you're thinking of going up against popular or powerful people, you've got to be absolutely sure that everything you say is accurate. This is no time for overstatement, nor for emotional arguments; if those are your weapons, you might as well stay home. Instead, make your case with clinical precision, and with all the information you can muster.

On two separate occasions during the Jimmy Carter administration, we at Mobil engaged in a public confrontation with the president. The issues were too technical to describe here in much detail, so I will merely outline the main points.

Our first confrontation with the White House, in the spring of 1979, came over the so-called windfall-profits tax. At the time, President Carter favoured a plan that would decontrol the price of both old oil (oil currently being produced) and new oil (oil not yet discovered). The president's plan also called for high, permanent taxes on both new and old oil.

The American Petroleum Institute, on the other hand, which generally represents the major oil companies, had a plan of its own. Like the Carter plan, the API proposal favoured decontrol of both old and new oil. But, not surprisingly, the institute strongly opposed the imposition of additional taxes. From our perspective, the API plan was certainly a good one. But in the world of pragmatic politics, it had no chance of success.

What was needed was a programme that was politically acceptable to the White House, but which would not saddle new oil with high taxes that would almost certainly discourage exploration. We attempted to fill this vacuum by putting forth our own plan, suggesting that the oil industry should forgo price increases on old oil, provided that new oil would be decontrolled and not burdened with additional new taxes.

In May of 1979, we launched a three-part offensive to publicize our plan. On the day of our annual meeting, William Tavoulareas, president of Mobil, delivered a major address that described our proposals in detail. The previous day, we had leaked the text of his speech to a *New York Times* reporter, so the plan was given major newspaper coverage the day it was announced. The third part of our one-day effort was a full-page ad describing the plan.

We also started working on a full-page ad in the *Times* that would list all four existing proposals – the president's, the American Petroleum Institute's, Mobil's, plus a fourth plan that was being considered by Congress. The ad was in the form of a scorecard – a chart that would show exactly how each of these plans would affect various constituencies.

One Friday afternoon in June 1979, just a few days before our ad appeared, a report came over the news ticker saying that because of our opposition to his plan, President Carter had called Mobil 'perhaps the most irresponsible company in the country.' The report did not quote the president directly, but cited information given to reporters by several participants who had attended a heated meeting between the president and various 'public-interest' groups. Jody Powell, the president's press secretary, would neither confirm nor deny the statement.

Not surprisingly, we were immediately flooded by calls from reporters, asking for our comment. Our response was to suggest that the reporters ask the White House if the statement could be confirmed. If so, we would then issue a statement of our own. But until there was a confirmation, we would make no comment.

All of the weekend newspapers carried the story, reporting Carter's attack as fact – which of course it was. Perhaps we should have responded even without White House confirmation. But it struck us as inappropriate to rely on third-party reports about what the president of the United States did or did not say about us.

Taking offence at Carter's allegation that we were 'irresponsible,' we ran the scorecard ad comparing the proposed programmes, with the following headline: 'Which of these four programmes do you think is the most responsible?' In another ad that we ran the same day, we described our attempts to establish the authenticity of the infamous quote, and then moved on to describe, once more, the important differences between our views and the president's.

Although we were displeased by Carter's characterization of

Mobil as 'irresponsible,' we were able to use his remark to call significant attention to our plan. We were also able to shift the debate from whether he actually called us 'irresponsible' to the more substantive question of what was to be done about the price of oil, both old and new. By his statement, the president allowed us to get the press and the public to focus on our programme in a way that we could never have done in more conventional circumstances.

After a summer marked by intense lobbying, Congress passed a bill that was fairly close to our own programme. There was a small tax on new oil, but it was a gradually decreasing one. In the end, the president signed a bill that closely followed the very principles he had earlier described as 'irresponsible.'

The following year we had another run-in with President Carter. In a statement in March 1980, the president once again singled out Mobil, this time charging that we had violated the price guidelines of the Council on Wage and Price Stability by $45 million. We strongly disagreed, and once again we took to the newspapers to state our case. The headline on our ad was 'Sorry, Mr President, you've been misled.' With our reputation at stake, we carefully went over the facts of the case to show that the president was indeed misinformed.

We subsequently reached a compromise with the Department of Energy: we would forgo certain future price increases to which we were entitled in exchange for an acknowledgement by President Carter that there was an honest difference of interpretation between us and the wage-price council over the technical interpretations of regulations. So despite our uncommonly bad relationship with the White House during the Carter years, we were able to gain at least a partial victory in both of these confrontations.

The lesson here may be not to be overly cynical about our system. For all its flaws, our system functions as a democracy. There are limits on power. And the truth does matter – even in politics.

When we first started to confront the president, some people actually believed we'd end up in jail! Almost everybody was convinced that we would suffer great penalties by taking on the White House. And almost everybody was wrong.

CONFRONTING CONVENTIONAL WISDOM

During the 1970s, the antibusiness climate of the day was greatly assisted by the periodic pronouncement of 'experts' who warned us all of the evils of large corporations, and of the urgency of limiting economic growth. We confronted these groups and individuals not because they posed an immediate threat to us, but because they provided the intellectual underpinnings and the philosophy for policies that we thought were both wrong and dangerous. The white-hatted experts who appoint themselves to represent the 'public interest' are generally few in number, but they create a ripple effect whereby their views soon find their way into universities, editorials, and even Congress. It's always easier to confront such ideas before they become too popular.

In 1972, the Club of Rome, a distinguished international group of scholars and businessmen concerned with the global problems affecting mankind, produced a thick and much-publicized report called *The Limits of Growth*. Drawing on computer projections, the report was, in effect, a doomsday forecast that maintained that the earth's resources were finite and in danger of being used up. Human society, argued the report, faced collapse within a century unless we could quickly establish a moratorium on the growth of population and industrial output. Unless the industrial nations adopted radically different life-styles, the report concluded, we would soon consume, pollute, and overpopulate ourselves out of existence.

The Club of Rome's report clearly touched a nerve, and intelligent and responsible people with varying political views were falling all over each other to endorse it. In part, this was because the report provided a measure of authority and credibility for an increasingly popular viewpoint: that growth and economic expansion were somehow dangerous to society, that big was bad, that small was beautiful.

To us at Mobil, however, these conclusions were both wrong and dangerous. First, they were based on the false premises that the earth's resources were finite and nonreplaceable. Somebody in the Club of Rome evidently forgot a basic law of physics – that matter can neither be created nor destroyed. Matter can only be changed. All matter, of course, is a potential energy source. When one source runs out, technology always unlocks a new one.

The second problem with the Club of Rome's conclusions was that they were essentially elitist. If the world were to follow these recommendations, the poor nations would have no chance to develop and to escape their abject poverty.

What did all of this have to do with oil? Not a great deal, so for us, this confrontation was purely discretionary. We were shocked and dismayed by the reflex reaction and complete acceptance that the report was generating. Even the business community was silent. Somebody had to speak up, so we did.

In response to the antigrowth point of view, we published an ad with the headline 'Growth is not a four-letter word.' We used most of our space for a long quotation from Anthony Crosland, a Labour member of the British Parliament. 'We must beware of some of our friends,' he noted.

> Their approach is hostile to growth in principle and indifferent to the needs of ordinary people. It has a manifest class bias, and reflects a set of middle and upper class value judgments. Its champions are often kindly and dedicated people. But they are affluent; and fundamentally, though of course not consciously, they want to kick the ladder down behind them. They are militant mainly about threats to rural peace and wildlife and well-loved beauty spots; but little concerned with the far more desperate problem of the urban environment in which 80 per cent of our citizens live.

For a time, the premises put forward by the Club of Rome were extremely fashionable. But only four years after the report appeared, the *New York Times* ran the following headline: 'Scholars Favour Global Growth. Members of Club of Rome Say Further Rise Is Needed to Fight World Poverty.' These days, we don't hear very much about 'limits to growth.'

CONFRONTING SELF-APPOINTED KEEPERS OF THE PUBLIC MORALS

Although we disagreed with their conclusions, we never believed that the Club of Rome was trying to undermine the fundamental tenets of capitalism. Theirs was essentially an economic and humanistic perspective rather than a political one. But the same could not be said of everybody who shared their views. Some groups and individuals, while clothing themselves in eminently respectable terms – as representatives of the consumer, for instance – have turned into self-appointed guardians of the public morals, whose goal is to achieve political power.

It's important to confront these groups, because despite their limited size, they do exert considerable influence on legislative bodies. Most of them, it should be acknowledged, operate from the purest of motives. The environmentalists, for example, care deeply about clean air, clean water, and the sanctity of the land – and who, indeed, could be against such things? And yet, during the 1970s, as corporate executives know all too well, the environmental impulse did untold damage to our nation's economy.

GROWTH DAY

Early in 1980, a coalition led by Ralph Nader announced that April 17 of that year would be 'Big Business Day,' an event that was to be marked by 150 antibusiness demonstrations around the country. The coalition's stated objective was to get Congress to pass the Corporate Democracy Act, a bill that would greatly complicate and slow down the efficiency of big business.

I was shocked that nobody in the business community seemed willing to take on Ralph Nader's coalition. Big Business Day, I decided, should not go unchallenged. After concluding that there should be a counterevent on April 17 called 'Growth Day,' I immediately contacted the Heritage Foundation, the conservative public-policy think tank in Washington, and enlisted their support.

I had in mind that we would proceed by using the very tactics that the Nader group had made famous. So we printed up buttons depicting a purple mountain, a blue sky, and the sun. We sent out press releases and printed up stationery. We lined up academic speakers all over the country. We contacted the media and asked for equal time – and got it. Without spending much time or money, we forced the Nader crowd to give up part of the turf.

The purpose of Growth Day was not only to counter the Nader event, but also to underscore some basic points about our economic system. We reiterated that growth was not a four-letter word, and that big did not have to mean bad. We pointed out that throughout our history, all of America's great successes had been closely tied to economic growth and expansion. We insisted that the then-fashionable idea of 'zero-growth' was a form of economic suicide.

By linking up with the Heritage Foundation, we created an important and viable coalition. And because we were filling a vacuum, our efforts received a great deal of press coverage. The press loves conflict, so even our minimum efforts received as much attention as the other side's. We could only imagine how the press and the television cameras would have covered the story had Big Business Day taken place unopposed.

COMMON CAUSE

Another example of discretionary confrontation came in 1984, when we took on Common Cause, the self-styled 'citizens' lobby,' on the issue of political-action committees. Common Cause was strongly opposed to PACs. As they saw it, the voice of the citizen was 'being drowned out by the ringing of PAC cash registers in Congress.' What they neglected to mention in their press releases was that out of sixty-five hundred lobbyists registered in 1983, Common Cause reported spending the third-highest amount, close to $2 million, in its attempts to influence Congress.

One general objective in this was to point out that the term *public interest* is in the eye of the beholder. Considering that the public agenda includes such diverse issues as the Equal Rights Amendment, abortion, the defence budget, airline financing, arms control, and many more, how could any one organization presume to speak for the public will?

On the specific issue of PACs, we pointed out that the first political-action committee was sponsored by the CIO back in 1943. More recently, PACs had been formed by environmentalists, feminists, and other single-issue constituencies. But now that corporations, too, were forming PACs, Common Cause wanted to draw the line. That sounded to us like a strong antibusiness bias, and we didn't want it to go unanswered.

In the effort to get rid of PACs, Common Cause lobbyists have advocated the public fincancing of elections. In their view, the concept of individuals freely joining with other individuals to support the candidate of their choice represented a serious abuse. In our view, the real abuse would have been to mandate the use of taxpayers' money to support candidates that many taxpayers might detest.

We made our points in a series of newspaper ads. I also debated Fred Wertheimer, president of Common Cause, before the National Press Club. 'I defy anybody,' I said in that forum, 'to prove a direct relationship between campaign contributions and legislative votes. And if anybody *has* such evidence, he ought to take it down to the Justice Department for possible prosecution.' At the time, Mobil's own PAC had raised a grand total of fifteen thousand dollars. Still, we saw the issue as one of constitutional principle on which we should take a stand.

With an issue of this type, the public you want to reach is the intellectual elite. After all, the survival of the individuals and the institutions we're talking about depends on the support of the intellectual community. Therefore, it is critical that your response is rigorous enough to participate in that debate. Your messages will need to show a high degree of thoughtfulness and articulate persuasion. Many intellectuals are open-minded enough to give a fair hearing to views they don't like – provided that those views are appropriately argued.

Now most people seem to believe that because people like Ralph Nader and groups like Common Cause are sacred cows, it's therefore dangerous, if not suicidal, ever to confront them. Our policy has been that when it comes to debating the issues, we are willing to take on anybody – and that we will not suffer by doing so.

CONFRONTING SOMEONE WHO'S OUT TO GET YOU

During my career, I've engaged in a fair number of confrontations. Until recently, I never had any evidence to suggest that our problems with any newspaper or television station were the result of a concerted campaign to damage the company I worked for. But with the *Wall Street Journal*, my colleagues and I came to exactly that conclusion. In response, we took the strongest steps we've ever taken with a journalistic organization.

But first, let me tell you about the five years of history that led up to our action. During that time, I had the opportunity to take a close-up look at the *Journal*. Most major newspapers are competitive places to work, but the *Journal* is especially so. Their newsroom is filled with young reporters who are under enormous pressure to move up the pyramid. On several occasions we have been approached by two or three journalists working on the same story, who have actually asked us not to talk to other reporters from the same paper. Moreover, the *Journal* has obviously opted for a kind of 'journalism' whose main interest is to increase circulation. In recent years, the paper has shown itself to be more interested in the gossip of business than in the business of business.

In recent years, the *Wall Street Journal* had kept up a constant drumfire of stories critical of Mobil and its top executives. More important, these stories contained numerous errors of fact and extensive use of unidentified and even fabricated sources.

Our problems with the *Journal* go back at least to 1979, when Paul Blustein, a *Journal* reporter, wrote a story about William Tavoulareas, who was then president of Mobil. Blustein's story dealt, in part, with a recently published article in the *Washington Post* that charged that Tavoulareas had improperly set up his son Peter in an English shipping concern that did business with Mobil.

The *Post*'s article had been so full of errors and distortions that Tavoulareas had taken the unusual step of suing that newspaper for libel. He eventually won the suit in a jury trial, although the verdict was later reversed by the trial judge. (As this book goes to press, the suit is on appeal.)

When Paul Blustein came to our offices to interview Tavoulareas, we told him that the meeting would be tape-recorded. We also made a point of giving him a copy of the tape. But apparently he didn't listen to it carefully enough, for his article on Tavoulareas included a number of inaccuracies and at least one incorrect quotation. We made a loud protest to the *Journal*, and after an unpleasant series of negotiations, they finally allowed Tavoulareas to write a letter, which they published in their news columns – a response they told us was unprecedented. If we hadn't made our own tape, it's unlikely that Tavoulareas's letter would ever have been printed.

Our next serious problem with the *Journal* occurred in 1982, when Mobil was involved in an unsuccessful attempt to acquire Marathon Oil. The *Journal*'s coverage of this transaction was filled with vague 'sources' – 'a Wall Street consensus,' 'most observers believe,' 'according to some observers,' 'a Marathon source says,' 'a Mobil lawyer,' and the like. A number of unattributed quotations and speculations were passed off as facts, with a result that was damaging to our reputation.

Now we at Mobil have grown accustomed to reading critical articles about us in the press. Still, this one broke new ground in its irresponsibility.We found the article so filled with errors that we sought a meeting with the *Journal*'s editors and publishers to discuss the relationship between our two institutions. I arrived at that meeting with a list of twelve statements, all drawn from that one article, that seemed to us either inaccurate or unfair. As I was in the middle of making the first of these points, Frederick Taylor, executive editor of the *Journal*, interrupted my presentation:

'Everything you're saying is bullshit,' he said. That was the end of my remarks.

One of my many points I never got to mention that day was the rather unusual line of questioning that was followed by a *Journal* reporter who had called me on the phone for an interview. At the time, our attempted acquisition of Marathon was tied up in Federal District Court in Ohio. 'Mr Schmertz,' said the reporter, 'how do you expect to get anywhere in this case when the judge is in Marathon's pocket?'

Now that was as loaded a question as I've ever heard, and I got angry. 'How do you know that?' I demanded. 'Do you have any evidence that your charge is true? Are you going to print your allegation in the newspaper?'

'It's common knowledge,' he replied.

'If you have any information along those lines,' I said, 'I hope you'll go right to the US attorney.' It's a good thing I had my wits about me that day, or I might have been entrapped into making a colourful quote I would have regretted.

During this same general period, Frederick Taylor made two public statements that suggested to us that he carried a strong bias against Mobil. The first of these statements came after Tavoulareas's victory over the *Washington Post*. Taylor was quoted in *Newsweek* as saying, 'It is a great commentary on our times when a jury finds for an oil company against a newspaper.'

When we read the statement, we wrote to Taylor and asked him whether the quote was accurate. 'I said it,' he replied, 'and you can use it.'

The statement disturbed us for two reasons. First, it was inaccurate. This had been a personal suit, brought by Mr Tavoulareas individually, and paid for with his personal funds. The jury did not 'find for' Mobil; Mobil was not even a party to the suit.

Second, Taylor's statement revealed a shocking bias. Even assuming that Mobil was involved in the case, Mr Taylor seemed to be saying that oil companies are so venal and so inherently evil that no matter what a newspaper says about them, they should never prevail in a court of law before a jury. If this wasn't bias, what was?

Frederick Taylor's second public statement was not intended for our eyes, but one of our employees happened to notice a highly unusual classified ad that appeared in the January 17, 1983, edition of the *Financial Times* of London:

PLEASE CALL
Will the author of the anonymous letter recently sent from the London area to Frederick Taylor, Executive Editor of The Wall Street Journal regarding a shipping concern, please call him collect? Business telephone is New York, Area Code 212, 555–7600. Home telephone is New Jersey, Area Code 201, 555–1952. Conversation will be treated in confidence.

It certainly seemed that Mr Taylor and his newspaper were going to extraordinary lengths to uncover information damaging to William Tavoulareas – and by extension, to Mobil. Now everybody knows that newspaper reporters and editors are continually receiving anonymous tips. But how often do the journalists go to the trouble of placing an ad in an attempt to contact these sources? And how often does the executive editor of a major newspaper get personally involved in the story – to the extent that he actually gives out his home number?

There was a third incident around that time that made us wonder about the *Journal*'s motives. On November 13, 1982, Paul Blustein saw Bill Tavoulareas at a Saint John's University social function. According to Tavoulareas, Blustein said that as a result of the news media's concern with Tavoulareas's victory over the *Washington Post*, any reporter who could 'get' Mobil or its executives would be a hero and would be substantially enhancing his career at the *Journal*. Moreover, because of the recent bitterness between Tavoulareas and Taylor, a reporter had a lot to gain by 'getting' Tavoulareas.

Before long, I received a call from Paul Blustein in which Blustein said that he now had new information alleging that 'Mobil had bailed out Peter Tavoulareas and Atlas, the company in which Peter Tavoulareas is a principal.' Blustein said that he had in his possession certain Mobil documents that had been given to him by a confidential source whom he would not identify. He told me that he wanted to interview Mr Tavoulareas to 'hear his side.'

I wrote a letter to Blustein and told him that Mr Tavoulareas categorically denied the allegation, that it was laughable, and that until Blustein produced material that supported these allegations, we saw no reason either to meet with him or help him in his research.

But Blustein continued to work on the story. Among other things, he called Mobil employees at home, late at night, and asked for the names of possible dissidents in the company. He also asked several employees to give him proprietary documents. One of these employees reported that Blustein asked him if he 'had heard any gossip concerning Mr Tavoulareas and his son, Peter, from individuals who may be "miscontent."' The employee said he hadn't.

Blustein also called most of our outside directors and asked several of them to give him proprietary documents about the company. One of the directors replied that his request was the most outrageous thing he had ever heard. Another said that he thought that it looked like the *Wall Street Journal* was sinking to the level of the *National Enquirer*. Blustein also called some of our suppliers, agents, brokers, and bankers with similar questions.

Throughout our troubles with the *Journal*, one of our biggest complaints had to do with what we believed were stolen documents. During our conversations with the paper, its reporters had described certain Mobil documents in their possession that we surmised to be either proprietary or forged. If the documents were proprietary, then, in our view, they were stolen goods. And if the *Journal* was making use of these documents for its own purposes and for profit, then, in our view, they were guilty of trafficking in stolen goods.

If, on the other hand, the documents in question were forgeries, this would discredit the newspaper's whole story. We asked for the return of these documents, but the *Journal* refused. Nor would they even show us copies of these documents so that we could examine them. In other words, they wanted us to answer questions about documents that they wouldn't even let us see.

The final episode in our relationship with the *Journal* came in mid-November of 1984. Earlier in the month, we had sent the paper two press releases on the same day. One was a fairly important story about the closing of a refinery in West Germany. The other announcement concerned Mobil's plans to build a $300-million office building in Chicago.

The *Journal* ran both stories. The refinery story was buried in an unrelated article about OPEC price cuts. The building story, on the other hand, was treated fairly prominently. Predictably, the *Journal*'s story focused not on the building itself, but on the fact that one of the leasing agents for the building was a firm that employed the son-in-law of Mobil's chairman, Rawleigh Warner, Jr. Mobil had been doing business with this firm for many years, but the *Journal* did not bother to mention that. To make matters worse, the article dredged up the unrelated and entirely discredited story about Tavoulareas and his son.

For us, this was the last straw. We responded by breaking off all relations with the paper. We called several of their reporters and told them that from now on, we would not answer their questions, on or off the record. Nor would we supply them with any data or grant any interviews. We also pulled our advertising from the paper.

Because corporations don't normally behave this way, our action caught a lot of people by surprise. As *Newsweek* put it, 'last week, instead of simply complaining to the *Wall Street Journal* about its coverage of the company, Schmertz and other Mobil executives took the extremely rare step of boycotting the newspaper altogether. No press releases. No interviews. No ads. The reason, says Schmertz, is that the *Journal* – thought by many to be the nation's premier business publication – is "not interested in business stories, but in gossip and innuendo stories."'

Now *that's* what I call accurate coverage.

When the news of our break with the *Journal* became public – and to the best of my knowledge, nobody at Mobil leaked it – some of our colleagues believed that we would be harmed by this seemingly impetuous action. We disagreed. In our view, the coverage of Mobil in the *Wall Street Journal* could not, realistically, get any worse.

Our decision to break off relations with the *Journal* was not a protest over the treatment of the two stories in 1984. It was, rather, the result of five years of unprofessional conduct on the newspaper's part. The *Wall Street Journal* had been sending us a powerful message – that it's editorial interests had more to do with gossip and innuendo than with useful business information. And so we concluded that it no longer served a useful purpose to continue our relationship.

These, then, are some case studies of confrontation from my own career. They show that confrontation is not always difficult, or unpleasant, or rude. And they show, I think, that while confrontation is certainly not a magic cure for all the potential problems that arise for the contemporary corporation, it is the best single technique for damage control that you can find. In today's business climate, confrontation is a tool you simply can't afford to be without.

The larger and the more important your institution, the more likely it is that both individuals and other institutions will be eager to attack you. For the most part, these attacks will not be against you personally, but against what your institution represents. It may be that your corporation is seen as an obstacle to social change. It may be that your institution is temporarily unpopular or vulnerable for any number of other reasons.

In our open and politicized society, there's no way to escape from this kind of vulnerability. Your only sensible choice is to confront your opponents and to stand your ground.

FOUR

Understanding the Press

OF ALL THE PUBLICS you'll be dealing with, the press is probably the most important – if only because it serves as the conduit to everybody else. The press is important for another reason, too: in recent years it has grown increasingly adversarial towards the people and the institutions it covers. As a result, business and other institutional executives have two choices: they can allow the press to do whatever it wants, or they can confront the press when confrontation is necessary.

In this chapter, I'll focus on what you should know about the press. In the following chapter, I'll discuss how to deal with the press to your best advantage.

By and large, American news organizations do a good job of reporting the news. At the same time, it's important that you understand some of the problems and the limitations of the news media, many of which could create serious problems for you. So if I concentrate in these pages on the negative side of the press, it's not because I hate the press or because I want to muzzle journalists. Rather, it's because what you don't know about the press can hurt you badly.

THE PRESS IS A BUSINESS

The first thing you should understand is that whatever else it is or claims to be, the press is fundamentally a business. Because the news media are so central to our lives, it's easy to forget that they are, in most cases, commercial ventures, rather than a public service. And as with any other commercial venture, the success or failure of a news organization is determined by the forces of the marketplace.

At the same time, the news media are different from other commercial ventures in that the relationship between their consumer sales and their profits is strangely indirect. In his book *The Media Monopoly*, Ben Bagdikian makes this point rather elegantly. What is it, he asks, that newspaper publishers actually do? They buy boiled pine trees, put them through a manufacturing process that turns them into newsprint, and fill that up with words and pictures. They then arrange the pages in a certain order and sell that arrangement as newspapers. It sounds simple enough, except for one curious fact: the publishers sell these processed pine trees for about one-third *less* than what they pay for them.

The difference, of course, is more than made up from advertising. In actual fact, most American newspapers make little or no money on news-stand sales and subscriptions. And yet they constantly strive to increase circulation – not for its own sake, but in order to generate more advertising, at higher rates (because the rates, of course, depend on the size of the readership). Circulation, then, is the bottom line – a fact that has a profound influence on how the news is presented.

In other words, merely reporting the news is not enough. If a newspaper or TV station is to stay in business, the news has to sell. A reporter who is working on a story is rewarded if his article generates a large readership, which is then translated into a larger circulation, which is then translated into more advertising pages and higher advertising rates.

Do these concerns really have an impact on the way that news is reported? Without question. In his book *Deciding What's News*, the social scientist Herbert Gans offers a particularly distressing example of this phenomenon. Gans claims that *Time* and *Newsweek* regularly attempt to improve the demographics of their readership by using tactics that are known to discourage low-income readers, including the occasional use of 'sex covers,' which are connected to feature stories on erotica, the pornography problem, sex education, and the like.

On the surface, of course, these covers are meant to increase news-stand sales. But according to Gans, they have another, more sinister purpose: they are also designed to encourage less liberal (which usually means less affluent) readers to cancel their subscriptions. (Gans also notes that there is no evidence that this policy actually works.)

The same commercial tendencies prevail – and more so – in

television news, where ratings are everything. On August 28, 1922, at 5:00 pm, a New York radio station aired the world's first commercial, and American broadcasting has never been the same. Today, the formula is very simple: the higher the ratings, the more you can charge the advertisers. This basic formula applies equally to every programme on commercial television, from *Saturday Night Live* to the evening news.

This simple fact of broadcast life was driven home to me a few years ago, shortly after Dan Rather had replaced Walter Cronkite on *The CBS Evening News*. I was having lunch with a producer from CBS, and I asked him how Dan Rather was doing in his new job. 'Thirty-one, twenty-six, twenty-three,' he replied. At first I didn't understand what he was talking about. Was Dan losing so much weight that these were his new measurements? It took a few moments before I realized that I was being offered the ratings scores for the evening news on CBS, ABC, and NBC, respectively. In other words, Dan Rather was doing very nicely.

The business priorities of news organizations have created a structure that inevitably distorts the product. What it boils down to is that the news has to be packaged in such a way that it sells. And if it doesn't sell, the people who report it and produce it will be out of a job. In other words, the news has to be interesting to a popular audience. Whenever possible, it has to be provocative and dramatic. If a story doesn't fall into these categories – and many business and political stories do not – it may not receive the attention it deserves.

REPORTERS ARE NOT SURROGATES OF THE PUBLIC

Let's imagine for a moment an America where 95 per cent of the population are white, 60 per cent are male, 93 per cent are college graduates, 78 per cent earn more than $30,000 a year, and 50 per cent profess no religion at all. While that certainly doesn't sound like the America I know, it does describe one segment of our population – our leading journalists and broadcasters.

The statistics I have just cited come from a study of the American media elite conducted in 1979 and 1980 by Professor Stanley Rothman of Smith College, and Robert and Linda Lichter of George Washington University. The research for the Rothman-

Lichter study consisted of 240 personal interviews with journalists and broadcasters from the *New York Times*, the *Washington Post*, the *Wall Street Journal, Time, Newsweek, US News & World Report*, the three major television networks, and PBS. In a word, the researchers found this group of 'opinion leaders' to be so strikingly different from mainstream America that they might as well have come from a different country.

Politically, the group is overwhelmingly Democratic – a fact that doesn't seem to shift along with the mood of the country. And so in 1972, for example, when 61 per cent of the American electorate voted for Richard Nixon, 81 per cent of the media elite voted for George McGovern.

There's more. In spite of massive amounts of foreign aid to underdeveloped countries, only 25 per cent of the media elite believed that the West had actually helped the third world. Closer to home, 40 per cent thought that the government should guarantee jobs for people. An astonishingly high number, 28 per cent, said that the United States needed a 'total overhaul.' More than 10 per cent of those surveyed – and more than 20 per cent of the *New York Times* employees – agreed that major American corporations should be nationalized. Finally, a full 90 per cent of the journalists in the survey believed that women should have the right to an abortion, while fewer than 10 per cent felt that homosexuality was wrong.

What are we to make of these intriguing statistics? Some observers have concluded that they constitute proof of a liberal conspiracy in the media. I disagree. Unlike some of my more conservative colleagues, I am not prepared to make the quantum jump from this study to conclude reporters as a group are antibusiness, or that they consciously allow their personal prejudices to creep into their objective reporting of the news. It's the product we have to consider, and not the motivation.

And while I would certainly prefer that our leading journalists were a little more diverse in their views, I do not object to the fact that they have biases. All of us, no matter how we earn a living, hold certain views about politics and society. The only difference is that in most occupations, so long as we perform the task for which we are being paid, those views don't really affect the way we perform our job.

But journalism is different. Its purpose, after all, is to sort out and present information so that readers and viewers receive an unbiased picture on which to base their own conclusions. And while nothing in the Rothman-Lichter study would suggest that reporters and editors are intellectually dishonest or that their reporting is inherently antibusiness, the study does raise the question of the unconscious impact of the reporter's views.

Take scepticism, a quality no journalist can do without. In a profession that calls for unravelling and then weaving together a diverse group of statements and situations into a coherent whole, a certain amount of scepticism is indispensable. At the same time, scepticism is unlike most of the other tools of journalism – tools like grammar and syntax, for example, which are discreet and objective skills. As a human quality, scepticism is conditioned by personal experience, by education, by social background. And so, for example, if a journalist happens to start out with a distrust of large institutions, it's almost inevitable that his scepticism will be skewed in the direction of that distrust, and that without even thinking about it, he will give more weight to anti-establishment views than to those of large corporations, big labour, or organized religion. In most cases the journalist does not intend to exercise such a bias. In all probability, he has no idea that this bias even enters into his reporting. But of course it does.

Now this whole matter of how reporters differ from the rest of us would not matter so much if members of the press did not insist upon viewing themselves as surrogates for the American public. Although this idea is most often left unsaid, from time to time I have heard people in the news business state it explicitly. 'To lie to the press on a public matter,' the columnist Dan Dorfman has said, 'is in effect to lie to the people.' Don Hewitt, the executive producer of *60 Minutes*, has made a similar point, although in keeping with the spirit of his show, he phrases it in more dramatic terms. Hewitt likes to say that the role of *60 Minutes* is to open the window and holler for the American people.

To be fair, if I worked for the news media, I too might be given to pious talk about how we were the surrogates of the public. Not only is this a warm and hugely appealing notion; it also grants the press an enormous amount of power. But as somebody who stands outside of the profession, I've always wondered where this idea came from in the first place. I understand perfectly well that journalists like to see themselves in this light, but by what authority can they do so? To put it more simply, if reporters are the surrogates of the public, who appointed them?

To hear the self-righteousness with which some journalists talk on this subject, you would think that there was some reference to this idea in the Bill of Rights. But there's nothing in the Constitution that says or even implies that the press is the representative of the people.

This is not to suggest that nobody is the surrogate of the people. It's just that in a democracy, being a surrogate is not a self-appointed position. Across the land, there are thousands of people who serve as our surrogates because they have been democratically elected to represent us in local, state, and federal governments. But nobody elected the media to represent the public. And certainly nobody asked them to be the self-appointed keepers of the public morals.

Be sceptical, then, when the press attempts to clothe itself sanctimoniously in the robes of the public surrogate. Individual reporters may be perfectly sincere when they strike this pose, but you should keep in mind that the value system of the press is that of a profit-making business rather than, say, a seminary.

DOES THE PRESS PROTECT THE PUBLIC?

Just as the press likes to see itself as the people's representative, news organizations like to present themselves as the protectors of the public. Anyone who takes a close look at the way the news is presented, especially on television, soon becomes aware of a familiar cast of characters. The names may change, but on business stories, at least, the basic constellation remains pretty much the same:

The Liberal Politician. Defender of consumer interests, protector of the environment, advocate of social justice, opponent of big business.

The Conservative Politician. In the pocket of big business and the entrenched interests. Defender of the rich.

The Social Activist. Often from a public-interest group. You can trust him. You can tell by the clothes he wears that he's not in it for the money.

Come to think of it, what *is* he in it for? Altruism? In part, perhaps. But it's rarely that simple. What about *his* economic or political motives? We rarely see reporting that speaks to those questions, even though the social activist may favour radical and fundamental changes in our political and economic system.

The Businessman. You can't trust him. He's motivated by greed for more profits, and cares about nothing else.

The Reporter. Where does he fit in? In the middle, naturally, where any reasonable person would be. The viewer or reader is supposed to be in the middle, too, properly sceptical of both sides – but especially of business. Why? Because business, after all, is driven by the profit motive. Its opponents may be a little naive, but at least they're pure.

The reporter is pure, too, except that he's supposed to be sensible and balanced. He is, after all, the impartial and trustworthy mediator between conflicting interests. But he's more than a judge; he's also like the old-time sheriff who brings the bad guys to justice. And the more the reporter can convey a sense that the world is a dangerous place, with untrustworthy people in positions of power, the more he enhances his image as a public protector. In other words, the press has a special interest in depicting allegedly dangerous people and allegedly dangerous situations. The more dangers the press can uncover, the more essential the press becomes.

And of course if the press is the great public defender, it would follow that other institutions in our society have a special obligation to the press. Now, clearly, those of us in corporate life do have specific obligations to certain publics. For example, we have specific obligations to our shareholders. We have other obligations to our employees, and still others to our customers. And without a doubt, we have a set of obligations to the government.

But to the press? As much as I like the press – and despite all my criticisms, I really do like the press – I don't believe that corporations have any special responsibility to Mr Sulzberger of the *New York Times*, or Mrs Graham of the *Washington Post*, or Mr Chandler of the *Los Angeles Times*. As far as I can tell, they're in business just like the rest of us.

MOST REPORTERS DON'T UNDERSTAND BUSINESS

While reporters often distort business stories to the detriment of the corporation they're describing, the problem usually isn't one of bias. In most cases, what's really at fault is the reporter's limited experience. Unfortunately, many journalists who report on the corporate world don't understand how that world works. Lacking the proper background, they tend to oversimplify and to look for heroes and villains. Many observers and commentators on the state of the press have noted that business and investigative reporters often resemble prosecutors or runaway grand juries or vigilantes from the Old West, convicting and hanging the guilty without a trial. Their only interest in business is to find a negative story that will get them promoted out of business into Woodward and Bernstein.

To be sure, many business reporters are familiar with the appropriate terminology and a few of the basic principles. But most of them lack the hands-on experience of negotiating, deal making, and the specific day-to-day techniques and decisions that are unique to each industry.

To the active executive, the dramatic moments of the business day constitute the joys, as well as the challenges, of being in business. But to the untrained eye, these same techniques may appear arcane, suspect, and disdainful, just as football must seem inordinately confusing for the first-time observer. Moreover, the financial rewards of successful business, especially when compared with the salaries of journalists, may well exacerbate these feelings.

Virtually every business leader in America has undergone the awkward and frustrating experience of being interviewed by a reporter who literally had no idea of what he, the executive, was talking about. There are reporters covering business stories – and this is more often true in television than in the print media – who do not understand such basic concepts as the difference between earnings and revenues, or between profits and profitability. There are reporters who seem not to understand the difference between owners and managers, and who fail to comprehend that the largest corporations in America are owned not by family dynasties or small groups of wealthy individuals, but by large and diverse groups of shareholders who are represented by pension funds, insurance companies, mutual funds, endowment funds, and the like. It's as if a sportswriter covering a football game did not know the difference between a fourth-down punt and a field goal.

Now it's also true that business stories are often fairly complex and technical. It's been said that the American economic system works brilliantly – except that nobody really understands it. And so perhaps a business reporter who doesn't know much about business can't really be expected to comprehend some of the stories he has to cover.

But wait. Why shouldn't a business reporter know very much about business? The reporter who covers the ballet knows something about dance. The food writer knows about restaurants and cooking. Why is it that the business reporter so often has no background in the area he covers?

The more I think about it, the more angry I become that sports journalism is so far ahead of business reporting. I haven't actually checked, but does anyone doubt that there are more statisticians and statistical researchers at ABC Sports than at ABC News? The analogy can be stretched still further. For example, would any sports fan accept a situation in which his home team received press coverage only when they lost? And yet the business coverage in many of our newspapers seems to operate by that very principle.

THE PROBLEM OF ACCURACY

Looking back, it's clear that Watergate represented a major turning point for American journalism. As everyone knows, Watergate ushered in a new era of investigative journalism, as would-be Woodwards and Bernsteins soon set their sights not only on government, but on a host of private institutions outside of government. Unfortunately, the energy crisis and other business stories did not fit very neatly into the Watergate framework.

But the heroic myth of the two courageous and enterprising reporters was too powerful to be stopped. The phenomenal success of *All the President's Men*, both the book and the movie, portrayed Bob Woodward and Carl Bernstein as golden boys who could do no wrong. The film, especially, lifted them into the realm of mythic media heroes – white knights sallying forth against crime and corruption.

In reality, however, the rush to beat the competition with ever-more-sensational exposés can – and did – lead to shoddy, libellous, and even fictitious reporting. When reporters turn into crusaders, they quickly lose their objectivity. And when that happens, truth is the first casualty.

Anybody who has ever been involved in a story that was reported on television or in the papers has learned how different an event can seem when it is portrayed by the media. To some extent, this is inevitable; take any group of people at the same event, and each of them will describe it a little differently. At the same time, growing numbers of Americans have become increasingly sceptical about what they read in the press or watch on the evening news.

This is not, of course, a new problem, and it certainly didn't start with Watergate. Some two centuries ago, Thomas Jefferson suggested facetiously that newspaper editors might wish to divide their paper 'into four chapters, heading the first, Truths; second, Probabilities; third, Possibilities; fourth, Lies.' And in a letter to John Norvell in 1807, Jefferson wrote, 'The man who never looks into a newspaper is better informed than he who reads them, inasmuch as he who knows nothing is nearer to truth than he whose mind is filled with falsehoods and errors.'

While errors and inaccuracies have been around as long as newspapers and magazines, the 1980s have been especially damaging to the reputation of print journalism. Perhaps the most famous incident was the 1981 episode in which Janet Cooke for the *Washington Post* won a Pulitzer Prize for a dramatic feature story about an eight-year-old heroin addict who turned out to be living in Ms Cooke's imagination.

To my mind, the real scandal here is that if her paper had not gone after the Pulitzer, Janet Cooke probably would never have been caught! But she should have been found out on Day 1, when her story was first proposed. Where were her editors?

Later, when the *Post* returned the prize, the paper ran an editorial assuring readers that 'more of the scepticism and heat that [we] traditionally bring to bear on the outside world will now be trained on our own interior workings.' That was an admirable statement, but readers had good reason to be sceptical. The *Post* got off easy. If only other corporations could dismiss their embarrassing mistakes with an editorial!

Soon after the Janet Cooke affair, Michael Daly, a star columnist for the *New York Daily News*, admitted that not everything he wrote for that paper had been completely accurate. The *New York*

Times was the next victim, when its prestigious magazine supplement published a 'true' story from Cambodia that was not only written in Spain, but was also plagiarized, in part, from a novel by André Malraux.

Newsweek's turn came in 1983, when the magazine ran a cover story on Hitler's 'diaries.' A week later, when there was good reason to doubt the authenticity of the documents, the magazine shamelessly contended that 'genuine or not, it almost doesn't matter in the end.' The week after that, *Newsweek* admitted that the diaries were a fraud.

In 1984, even the venerable *New Yorker* suffered some embarrassment when, despite the magazine's elaborate and famous fact-checking department, Alastair Reid, one of its veteran foreign correspondents, revealed that for years he had been inventing some of the details in his reports from abroad.

To be fair, these disclosures do not necessarily mean that the press is growing less accurate. It may just be that the problems are now more apparent. But if there are more inaccuracies now than in the past, here again Watergate may be the smoking gun. Ever since Watergate, many young reporters have started out by assuming the worst about the people or institutions they have been sent to cover, and have then tried to make the facts fit the theory.

Unfortunately, the problem is not confined to the larger city papers. As the editor of a tiny newspaper in Broomfield, Colorado, told *Time* magazine: 'Every kid I get out of journalism school wants to have some major exposé under his byline. Sometimes they cannot accept the fact that something is not crooked.'

But it's too simple to blame Watergate for all of the inaccuracies that are published and broadcast every day. Part of the problem stems from the inability of some reporters to understand fully the story they're working on, a situation that may result from time pressures or from a simple lack of experience and training. Another reason for mistakes is that well-meaning reporters are routinely given wrong information – sometimes intentionally, often not – and don't always have a way to correct the mistakes. Editors will rationalize this by admitting that they don't always print the truth, because they only print what people tell them – and people sometimes lie.

Even when there is a way to check the accuracy of a story, not every journalist takes the time and trouble to get involved in the less glamorous side of journalism. And yes, there are a handful of reporters who knowingly write false or incomplete information for their own political or personal reasons. But whatever the reasons, even the best newspapers publish a fair amount of inaccurate information. 'Doctors bury their mistakes,' goes the old newsroom proverb, 'and lawyers send theirs to jail. Only journalists sign their mistakes and print them on the front page.'

THE PROBLEMS OF STOLEN DOCUMENTS

To my mind, one of the most disturbing trends in the press is the widespread use of stolen documents. Journalists invariably describe such material as 'leaked,' but to me that's just a euphemism for the theft of private property. When a reporter from a news agency asks a source to give him private documents – material that will help the news agency in its ongoing profit-making business – doesn't that constitute a request to steal? By insisting on the legitimacy of this practice, reporters are asking for a right that is denied to everyone else in our society.

Some reporters believe they have the right to examine all government documents. After all, they reason, the government is nothing more than the people, and the people have a right to know. I don't happen to buy that argument.

But even if reporters do have the right to government documents, on what basis are they entitled to the documents of a corporation? Corporations are required by law to file certain disclosures and announcements. But once we've complied with those regulations, where is it written that we have to go beyond them to satisfy the needs and whims of reporters? As far as I'm concerned, the public's 'right to know' does not extend into my desk drawer. Business executives have no obligation to provide the press with material that's private or proprietary. Moreover, if they do provide such material, they should be fired. Unfair tactics may sell newspapers and boost ratings, but they have severe consequences for the image and credibility of the press.

THE PROBLEM OF UNNAMED SOURCES

Even a cub reporter knows that sources who refuse to be identified are notorious for passing on 'information' whose primary purpose is not to enlighten, but to advance a particular personal or political agenda. And yet, perhaps because of the enormous public interest in Woodward and Bernstein's 'Deep Throat' (a character whose very existence may have been fabricated), some reporters apparently feel that the use of unnamed sources makes them look more powerful or glamorous – which may be still another consequence of Watergate. If the press really wants to see itself as the surrogate of the people, it should provide the people with enough information to evaluate a source's credibility, his motivation, and his competence. This is especially true when the source is used to illustrate or document adverse information about an individual or an institution.

Another problem with unnamed sources, or 'blind quotes,' is that there can rarely be any guarantee that the quotation in question is accurate or even authentic. In some cases, the use of an unnamed source is simply a socially acceptable way of introducing a fabricated quotation into a story. In *The Other Side of the Story*, a fascinating account of his years as press secretary during the Carter administration, Jody Powell discusses the widespread use of 'blind quotes' by the Washington press corps, noting wryly that 'few journalists deny that this takes place, although I could find none who would admit to doing it themselves.'

Powell goes on to describe how, early in the Carter administration, *Newsweek* interviewed National Security Adviser Zbigniew Brzezinski as part of a political story. When the text of the interview arrived in New York, the magazine's editor rewrote some of Brzezinski's comments to adhere more closely to the theme of the article. They sent the revisions to Brzezinski and asked if he would approve them for use for publication.

Brzezinski refused. His position was that *Newsweek* could use what he actually said, or they could use nothing at all.

After describing the episode, Powell makes a disquieting observation: 'If the source had been a lower-level official,' he writes, 'speaking anonymously instead of on the record, one cannot help but wonder whether any attempt would have been made to seek approval for the doctoring.'

SULLIVAN AND THE PROBLEM OF LIBEL

One of my biggest concerns about the press these days is that under the current laws, any prominent businessman stands a good chance of being libelled with impunity. Let's take a few moments to understand how this situation became so serious.

Back on March 29, 1960, a group of civil-rights supporters and clergymen took out a full-page ad in the *New York Times* that was critical of law enforcement officials in Alabama. Although the ad did not mention any of these officials by name, it did list examples of police harassment – examples that, unfortunately, contained some factual errors. Several of the law enforcement officials, including L. B. Sullivan, the Montgomery police commissioner, instigated a libel suit against the *Times* and the four black clergymen whose names had appeared on the list of signatories. The case was tried by a staunchly segregationist judge in Alabama, and, with his blessing, the jury returned a verdict awarding Sullivan half a million dollars.

Four years later, in an unanimous decision, the Supreme Court threw out the earlier state court verdict. In its ruling, the Court set forth a new and more onorous standard of proof for libel cases. From now on, said the Court, public officials could recover damages from news organizations only if they could prove that false and defamatory statements about them were made with 'actual malice' – a term defined by the Court as statements known by the publisher to be false, or made by the publisher with reckless disregard as to whether or not they were false.

Until *Sullivan*, the burden of proof in these cases was on the news organization, which had to prove that its allegations were true, made in good faith, and without malice. But after *Sullivan*, the burden of proof shifted to the plaintiff. A public official who felt he was libelled now had to prove, first, that an allegation about him was untrue; second, that it had defamed him; third, that this defamation had damaged his reputation; and fourth, that the publisher of the statement either knew or had reason to believe that the story was untrue.

Today, in the wake of *Sullivan*, a public figure has little chance of winning a libel case against a news organization unless he can show that the reporter's notes said, 'I know that this story is a lie, but I'm going to use it anyway.' Because of *Sullivan*, it is actually in the reporter's interest not to do too much research when working on a potentially libellous story, and not to retain his notes.

For over twenty years, the press has enjoyed the fruits of *Sullivan*, which allows it to publish or broadcast false or damaging statements about a public official – unintentionally, of course –

without any liability or punishment. Because the burden of proof has shifted to the plaintiff, the press, for all practical purposes, has become immune from prosecution.

Even so, in recent years the number of libel suits against the press has been steadily growing. In the vast majority of cases that are decided upon by juries, those juries, acting on their moral impulses and on common sense, have found for the plaintiffs. But the judges, following *Sullivan*, as they must, have reversed these decisions or substantially reduced the awards. So among other problems caused by *Sullivan*, we now have a situation where the law is out of step with the views of the true representatives of the public – the juries.

Today, more than twenty years after *Sullivan*, there is a general willingness to take another look at the effects of this momentous decision. In the wake of the lawsuits instigated by Generals Westmoreland and Sharon against CBS and *Time* magazine, respectively, even the press is having second thoughts. James Squires, editor of the *Chicago Tribune*, not long ago told *Time* that 'Sullivan helped make us less conscientious and considered. It also made us overconfident and cocky.' And a 1985 editorial in the *Washington Post* stated that 'the law of libel, as it is now developing, works exceedingly badly. . . . In retrospect, it is evident that the Supreme Court set the law moving on the wrong course in the memorable *Sullivan* case two decades ago.'

The news organizations, arguing against any change in the libel laws, have always cited the First Amendment. But where are the civil libertarians when the reputation of a public figure is damaged? In becoming a public person, does one give up his rights as a citizen?

Another argument cited by news organizations is that Congress is powerless to interfere with the freedom of the press. But libel is a clearly established tort, which means that Congress has every right to enact legislation to deal with it.

Other countries with long traditions of press freedom rooted in their constitutions have no equivalent to *Sullivan*, and see no need for it. A few years ago, the English appointed a royal commission to determine whether they should adopt *Sullivan*. The commission rejected the idea, but the English press remains as vigorous and aggressive as ever.

Despite its considerable moral justification at the time, the *Sullivan* decision has been a poor law. Consider the case of

General Ariel Sharon of Israel, for example, who was able to prove that statements about him in *Time* were false and defamatory. And yet, because Sharon was unable to prove 'actual malice,' *Time* was not required to do anything to rectify the situation.

According to the press, the greatest danger in the abolition of *Sullivan* is that news organizations would be threatened with bankruptcy every time they made an honest mistake. But that doesn't have to happen. Where the reputation of a public official has been unfairly damaged, the new law might require nothing more than a simple but prominent retraction – or access to the news medium for the plaintiff to set the record straight in words of his own choosing – in addition to the payment of the plaintiff's legal fees. Or perhaps the plaintiff should have a choice. If he preferred to have his case tried under *Sullivan*, he would have to prove actual malice. But if he succeeded, he would then be awarded a considerable judgment.

If Watergate is one large part of the problem, *Sullivan* is another. Unless we find a way to attach some punishment to lying, and some premium to telling the truth, the abuses of the press may well grow worse before they get better. Currently, as a result of *Sullivan*, there is a real risk in reaching the top. In the event you are libelled, you will have no way to protect against damage to your reputation unless you can bear the enormous financial and emotional burden of proving actual malice. The legacy of *Sullivan*, then, is that being a journalist means that never having to say you're sorry.

HOW THE PRESS RESPONDS TO CRITICISM

Over the past two decades, our society has been strengthened by undergoing an intense period of public scrutiny, a process in which the press has certainly played a major role. These days, people expect more from companies than dependable products and services. They also expect corporations to be socially responsible, to be good public citizens, to be sensitive to the environment, and to be candid in dealing with the public and its surrogates – both elected and self-appointed.

And it's not only business institutions that have undergone these changes. Other institutions in our society, institutions of government, education, religion, and entertainment, have been affected by a similar transformation. And here, too, the press has played a major role in bringing about these changes.

In some cases, journalists merely give expression to the mood of the times. In other cases, reporters actively help to create these changes. Our free and critical press has helped foster a healthy scepticism towards all of society's institutions, and as a result of that scepticism, they are all more accountable and more responsible.

Well, almost all. As the major institutions of society have undergone major reforms in the past quarter of a century, there's been one conspicuous exception: the press itself.

When you stop to think about it, it's amazing how long the press has managed to avoid public scrutiny. Whenever those in the news media have been challenged, they have grown righteously indignant. Basking in the glow of Watergate, members of the press have refused to acknowledge that they are ever on the wrong track. Never mind that reputations have been tarnished by untrue stories. Never mind that bad laws have been passed because of zealous crusading that hasn't always portrayed the whole picture. The rush into print or onto the air with ever-more-sensational scandals and conspiracies was, for a time, all-consuming. In the short run, it sold newspapers and it sold advertising. But in the long run, the public will ultimately be tired of it.

Now, in view of the various problems I have cited, not to mention the series of public embarrassments that the press has suffered in recent years, you might expect that the news organizations would be showing a certain degree of humility. Unfortunately, that's not the case. When the press is attacked, it responds in two predictable ways. First, it goes into a circle-the-wagons, paranoid posture, in which anybody who dares to criticize is seen as the incarnated spirit of Spiro Agnew. The second predictable response is a lot of pious talk about the First Amendment.

But stonewalling the critics and crying wolf about the First Amendment are not going to help the press solve its image problem. And when a service industry like the press has an image problem, it can be very serious. So far, at least, the press has done little to improve its image. While the public sees the press as increasingly fallible, the press continues to project an aura of infallibility. And while the public sees the press as increasingly arrogant, the press continues to project the image of an underdog.

I have many friends in the news media, and over the years I have tried to raise some of these issues with them. But I have repeatedly found that the journalists and editors who work for newspapers and television networks generally don't like to discuss morality with me. To be more precise, they're perfectly happy to discuss morality with me – so long as it's my morality. Their morality, it seems, is off-limits. While reporters and editors feel free to discuss and investigate the morality of business executives and their institutions, the process doesn't seem to work both ways. Members of the press criticize corporate America every day. But whenever somebody from the business world criticizes the press, the news gatherers react as though we're trying to close them down.

Ideally, of course, people like me shouldn't have to criticize the press. The press, after all, feels perfectly free to criticize every other institution in our society. Why should members of the media be so reluctant to criticize or examine themselves?

Fortunately, there are at least some tendencies in the right direction. As mentioned, a growing number of newspapers are now making use of ombudsmen – independent observers and commentators who are free to criticize, in print, the paper they work for. And then there are publications like the *Washington Journalism Review* and the *Columbia Journalism Review*, which make a real attempt to cover the press and to blow the whistle on bad journalism. But in the end, these publications are relatively small, and their impact, unfortunately, is limited.

Besides, press criticism is too important to be relegated to the journalism reviews. Most major newspapers cover books, movies, concerts, dance, and television. Some newspapers even cover electronic journalism. But print journalism rarely covers itself, and electronic journalism rarely deals with *any* journalism. This is especially unfortunate because journalists are forever frustrated by having to report on stories and institutions about which they know very little. Here's a splendid opportunity for them to delve into topics about which they already know a great deal.

If a public official is incompetent on the job, you can count on learning about it from the news media. But if the same holds true for a respected journalist, how will the public know about it? Back in the Truman administration, when the president was vacationing in Florida, one of the regular reporters was too drunk to file a story. So three of his colleagues, each acting on his own, deciding to help out their friend by sending carbons of their own stories to his editor. The following day, the editor wired back: 'I like the second version of your story best.'

It's an amusing story, of course, but it also has a darker side, for it shows the double standard by which reporters operate. Jody Powell tells of a more recent example. During his four years as President Carter's press secretary, Powell came to the conclusion that Jack Anderson, the syndicated columnist, was 'dangerously unreliable.' After leaving the White House and becoming a journalist himself, Powell was surprised to learn that his opinion of Jack Anderson was in fact shared by most of the respected reporters in Washington. And yet none of these eminent practitioners ever criticized the reporting of their errant colleague.

Why should reporters enjoy special privileges of immunity that they are unwilling to grant to public officials? So long as the press is going to report on the faults and the private lives of public figures, why should prominent journalists – who are sometimes better known than top officials – be treated any differently? If, for example, it's important to tell the public that staff members in the White House are using cocaine, isn't it also news that cocaine may be widely used at the *Washington Post*?

This is not a theoretical argument, as the question came up not long ago on *The CBS Morning News*. In June 1984, when Bob Woodward of the *Post* was promoting his book on John Belushi, he was interviewed by Diane Sawyer. There was some discussion about the use of drugs in Hollywood (a major topic of Woodward's book), and then Diane Sawyer asked Woodward about drug use in Washington.

Woodward replied: 'A number of people have said to me – and I guess maybe I should be specific – that there are probably forty people at the *Washington Post* who use cocaine regularly.' Woodward said he could not confirm the story, but that he had heard it from people who worked for the paper. Believe me, if such a story had been circulating about any other prominent insitution in Washington, Bob Woodward would have had a couple of reporters at the door within the hour.

As I see it, the news media want to have things both ways. On the one hand, they expect and enjoy the trappings of power. But on the other, they refuse to accept the responsibilities and risks that go with the territory. What this means is that if you have a problem with the press, you can't expect that the press itself – or anyone else, for that matter – is going to come to your rescue.

These, then, are my principal beefs about the news media. Again, these complaints don't mean that I'm a foe of the press, or that I believe that reporters are biased or incompetent or untrustworthy as people. But I do think that certain problems are part and parcel of how the press currently operates, and that anyone who deals with the press should do so with open eyes. In the following chapter, we'll get down to specifics.

FIVE

How to Deal with the Press

IN THE PREVIOUS CHAPTER, I tried to cut away some of the mystery and mystique that surrounds the press by looking closely at the sources of its power and at some of its operating principles. I wish I could tell you, in this chapter, how to eliminate the various problems I'll be discussing, but that's not always possible. At the same time, if you're willing to confront the press head-on, challenging its practices, its assumptions, and its representatives, you can become a participant in the process, rather than a victim.

WHAT YOU SHOULD KNOW ABOUT TELEVISION NEWS

The most important thing you should understand about television news is that it has far more to do with television than with news.

In 1960, only a quarter of a century ago, less than half of the homes in American had television sets. Today, the figure is virtually 100 per cent. And while there are still people who depend on newspapers to know what's going on, the great majority receive their information from TV news. It's been estimated that there are more viewers of *each* of the network evening news shows than there are readers of all American morning newspapers combined!

This is not the place for an exhaustive list of the problems of television shows, but I will mention a few of the most serious. First, there is the problem of time. With up to a dozen stories crammed into a twenty-five-minute programme, there is rarely enough airtime to do justice to any single story. As Walter Cronkite once pointed out, television inadvertently distorts information and events 'when we all are forced to fit 100 pounds of news into the one-pound sack we are given to fill each night.'

The second problem is that television is a visual medium – a limitation that places enormous constraints on what constitutes news. If an issue or an event can't be easily filmed or photographed, it might as well not have happened. If a complex story is not visually exciting, television won't touch it.

On the other hand, television news is always interested in stories involving drama and conflict. When a TV journalist wants to interview me, I generally assume one of two things: either the story he's working on is hostile to me or my company, or else he wants to use me to attack somebody else. When a print reporter calls, I make no such assumptions.

A third problem is that television is still a relatively new form of communications that has not yet been fully mastered even by the people who work in it. As a result, more creative energy goes into the medium than into the message. 'The best minds in television news,' Charles Kuralt once wrote in the *Los Angeles Herald-Examiner*, 'are thinking more about packaging and promotion and pace and image and blinking electronics than about thoughtful coverage of the news.'

But perhaps the biggest problem, as we saw in the previous chapter, is that like everything else on television, the news is produced with the ratings in mind. By now, the public has come to accept this, but when it comes to the news, I don't see why we should have to. For years NBC lagged behind its two competitors, and it came to be known as the number-three network. Compare this to the newspapers in New York: how many people really know, or care, about the relative circulations of the *Times*, the *Post*, the *News*, or *Newsday*?

On television, a single point in the ratings can often mean a million dollars in extra income. But ratings go beyond money, for they also measure power and prestige. Monday mornings at the major networks are reminiscent of a crowd at a football game waiting to break into the chant 'We're number one!' The ratings game is really a macho, locker-room syndrome in which victory translates into the better tables at New York's tonier restaurants, more favourable mention in the gossip columns, and, of course, job security. A morning or evening news show in the number-two or number-three position will be subject to endless speculation about its format, its set design, and its anchors. Needless to say, this carnival atmosphere is hardly conducive to efficiency and responsibility in the newsroom.

There is, however, at least one common objection to television news that I do not agree with. Some of my colleagues complain that television news doesn't deal with business or economic news, but here I must dissent. As I see it, there's actually a great deal of business news on television. Local news, for example, is filled with stories about business – especially arson, drugs, gambling, and prostitution. Unfortunately, that's a pretty one-sided view of 'business,' and local news has yet to discover the law-abiding side. The national news is a little more sophisticated. Its coverage of business concentrates on the misery and the suffering that business and the economy are invariably causing society.

Is it any wonder that the average business executive is reluctant to be interviewed on television? Maybe it's because when he turns on the evening news, he finds that the two-hour interview taped earlier that day has been boiled down to twenty seconds. Of that the editing has turned him into a blunt, crude stereotype of a businessman, like the money-grubbing cardboard figures on *Quincy*.

Unless he's awfully naive, our executive is well aware that when the interview is over, someone he doesn't know is going to be cutting up bits of tape and running them together again, and that the results may not even come close to what he was trying to say, or may even have said. That's why a growing number of executives refuse to be interviewed at all, unless the interview is live. That way, 'creative' editing cannot distort what they say. For if a businessman is harmfully misquoted, or his reputation is damaged, he has little recourse outside of the courts.

Unfortunately, these problems are equally true of both national and local news. In general, local news reporting tends to be worse, in part because there is more time to fill, and in part because the local TV journalists are generally less skilled and less experienced than their network counterparts.

But in spite of everything I have just said, it's critical that you not be afraid of television news and TV reporters. It's not that there's no reason to be afraid; but your fear will work against you. If you allow yourself to be intimidated by the press, and if you allow the press to use unfair techniques, the results can indeed be disastrous. But that doesn't have to happen.

Always keep in mind that although it may not seem that way, you actually have as much power as the reporter. Now, it's true that many reporters will try to be the social arbiters of their relationship with you. They may approach you in a quasilegal way. They may approach you as an adversary. They may approach you as your friend – or through a friend. But you don't have to reciprocate on their terms. When you're dealing with journalists, it's best to be professional, discreet, and cordial – just as you would in any other business relationship.

Because the reporter needs your participation to do the story, you are in a position to set up conditions that are favourable to you as the price for your participation and cooperation. Before you agree to be interviewed, consider what you'll need to protect yourself and to feel comfortable. Most reporters will be sensitive to your needs and requirements – so long as you know what they are and take the trouble to make them clear.

What it comes down to is that you have options. You can negotiate. You can take steps to protect yourself and to create a more level playing field – which is what this chapter is all about.

WHAT TO DO WHEN *60 MINUTES* CALLS

The so-called television magazine shows are a curious hybrid, made up of elements of the old *Life* magazine, the old *Vanity Fair*, and a dash of the *National Enquirer*. On the surface, these shows fall into the category of 'news.' After all, they are produced under the auspicious rubric of the network news departments. Moreover, the reporters and anchors on these shows often have impressive journalistic credentials. But the blunt fact is that television magazine programmes are entertainment shows.

To be sure, these shows pretend to investigate real news stories. But in actual fact, they are highly structured, very expensive, and carefully edited productions that appeal not to the viewer's intellect, but to his emotions. The magazine shows go to great lengths to satisfy the audience's apparently insatiable curiosity about the rich and the famous, as well as the considerable satisfaction they derive from seeing the villain – often a business executive – apparently caught with his hand in the cookie jar.

In their attempts to do investigative journalism, the magazine shows act like a kind of people's court. For this is where business executives are routinely accused, indicted, prosecuted, convicted, and punished with astonishing speed. In the world of the magazine shows, people in business are guilty until proven innocent.

As we've already seen, the networks won't let me, a businessman, buy time on their show to give my views. But when Mike Wallace shows up at my door with a TV camera and I don't let him in, the camera rolls on and *60 Minutes* shows Herb Schmertz slamming the door on any kind of discussion of his business practices. On television, when you don't submit to questioning, you're guilty. The conclusion? You must have something to hide. This may be why John McNulty, vice-president of public relations at General Motors, recently said that '*60 Minutes* is to journalism what *Charlie's Angels* is to criminology.'

In my view, the popularity of these magazine shows will soon come to an end. By the 1990s, the current crop of these shows will no longer be on the air. These programmes are formulaic, and by now the public has figured out the formula. When the ending is known in advance, there's not much room for suspense.

The advice that follows is based on my experience in dealing with *60 Minutes* and other television magazine shows. While *60 Minutes* is the most popular of these programmes – for years, in fact, it was the most popular show on television – most of the information in this section applies to any TV interview.

My advice is divided into three distinct time frames. The initial period begins when you are first contacted by the show. The second period begins when you decide whether or not you'll participate. The third period begins if and when you actually do the interview.

THE FIRST PERIOD

A producer or a reporter from *60 Minutes* calls to request an interview – either with you, or with somebody from your company. What should you do?

At first, nothing. Don't make any decisions until you have to. At this point, your goal is simply to collect as much information as possible about the segment they're planning. You have the right to ask as many questions as you wish, and now, before you decide whether you'll participate, is the time to ask them.

It's generally safe to assume that the segment involving your organization will be either highly sceptical or down-right hostile. And yet the person who contacts you from the show will probably be very friendly – which is how you should act toward him. But don't be misled. While this warmth may turn out to be genuine, it's more likely to be a calculated strategy to induce you to cooperate.

From the very start, take copious notes on every conversation you have with representatives of the show. Keep a written record of every question you ask – whether or not you receive an answer. Some of your questions might be:

- Exactly what is the segment about?
- What is its thesis?
- Whom do you want to interview from our organization, and why?
- What areas do you want to cover in that interview?
- Who else will be interviewed on the segment?
- What documents do you have?
- Who are the reporter and the producer for this segment?
- When is the show scheduled to air?

Of course, the mere fact that you ask these questions does not mean that you will be given the correct answers – or any answers, for that matter. On the other hand, you may learn a great deal. In either case, your notes should show exactly what you asked, and what, if anything, you were told.

Once you've learned everything you can about the show, explain to the person who called you that you'll discuss his request with your management, and that you'll call him back with an answer.

At this point, you might want to write the producer a letter saying something like this: 'Based on our conversation earlier today, the following represents my understanding of what the segment is about. Would you kindly confirm that I have understood you correctly?' The purpose of this letter is to serve notice that you are holding the producer to a high standard. If you have not been told the real purpose of the segment, your letter could lead the producer to rectify this.

At this point, you should call a meeting of your top people and discuss how you'll respond to the request. In most cases, you'll have to do some educated guessing: What story are they going after? What story *might* they be going after? To be safe, assume that the producer is planning to do the worst possible story from your point of view, and plan accordingly.

You might also want to discuss whether the person they want to interview is effective on television. If he isn't, you could suggest that they interview somebody else. Or you may want to give your person a crash course in television interviews. Fortunately, this is a skill that can be learned quickly with the help of a qualified consultant.

Another item you have to consider is whether, if you decline to be interviewed, they would prepare the segment without you. And if they did, what would be the consequences? The person who contacted you may have implied that they're doing the segment anyway, but this could be a bluff. They may be trying to build a case that would be impossible to make without the participation of your company. On more than one occasion I've said no to a request for a television interview, and by a remarkable coincidence, the segments in question were never aired.

The producer, of course, will try to convince you that if your organization doesn't participate, people will think you have something to hide. There is some truth to this, especially when they announce that 'the XYZ Company refused repeated invitations from us to refute these charges and to present their own point of view.' But there are also times when appearing on the show is even worse than not appearing.

What are some reasons not to participate? Because you don't want to be part of a loaded-deck, anti-intellectual entertainment show that masquerades as news. Or because you know that the interviewer is out to get you. Or because you're convinced that your story is complex, and that television will oversimplify it in a way that is adverse to your interests. Or because you perform poorly on television and you suspect that no matter how valid your case is, you'll look guilty. Or because to answer the questions will mean having to reveal proprietary information. In other words, your job here may be to select the lesser of two evils.

Even as you're making your decision, there's more research to be done. It's useful to know the track record of the people you're dealing with, so somebody from your organization should be reviewing the work of the producer and the journalist who are working on this particular segment. Beyond that, perhaps somebody in your organization knows an employee of the show who might be willing to fill you in as to their real intentions.

The point here is that information gathering is a two-way street. The press can do it, but so can any other business organization. You too can be a reporter, and just as the show is investigating your company, you can do the same to them. The more information you have, the more easily you can make the right decision. In the event that your investigative reporting uncovers any evidence that the planned segment will be biased or ill-informed, write a letter of protest.

During this period and the negotiations that follow, don't assume that you have no rights in this process. That's what the producer may want you to think, but don't buy it. Instead, act as if the segment were as much yours as theirs. Remember, they approached you and asked you to help them by participating. They did not call you because they love you and want to put you on television.

When you've completed your homework, call the producer. Even though you still haven't made your final decision, strike a positive note. Say that you want to find a way to participate, but that you need a little more information:

- You might ask him to send you a letter describing the show's thesis, and how your organization fits into it. If he won't, ask him at least to confirm the points you made in your earlier letter.
- You might request copies of any document they plan to question you about. If they refuse, ask them to explain why. You might say, incredulously, 'You mean you're going to ask us to comment on documents that we can't even see?'
- If you have reason to believe that the reporters are in possession of documents that may be private or proprietary, and were taken from your company, ask for their return. Raise the possibility that the documents may be incomplete, out of date, or even forgeries. If you think they may be forgeries, ask the producer to prove they're genuine.
- You might inquire as to the content and the source of any negative statements that they plan to use about your organization or its leadership, especially if you will be asked to respond to these statements. If the criticism comes from an anonymous source, ask the producer if he has considered the credibility and the motivation of that individual. Ask how the public is to be reassured that the source is objective and accurate.
- You might say that you're willing to be interviewed if the interview is unedited. Explain that you're willing to limit the interview to a specific amount of time to conform to their needs. This request will be refused, but here again you're serving notice that you understand that the very structure of the show could work against you, and that you're wise to such tricks.

- Ask how long the interview will last. Ask if the producer is willing to present questions or to outline the subject matter in advance so that your person can be prepared for any technical answers.
- If the subject of the segment is complex or technical, you might offer the possibility of an off-camera background briefing by your own technical people. Whether or not they accept your offer, you've gained something. If they say yes, you have a real opportunity to offer them important and relevant information that may prevent errors on the show. Make an audio tape of the briefing, and later, send a letter confirming the major points that were raised during the session. Say that you assume this material will be included in the show.

If they reject the idea of the briefing, you have at least put them on notice that the subject is complex and potentially difficult. As a result, they may be more careful in their approach. Another possibility is that your offering the briefing will lead them to conclude that the subject is too big or too complicated for them to handle in the short amount of time they have available.

THE SECOND PERIOD

By this time, you can no longer postpone your decision.

If you decide to say no, there are several ways to proceed. One option is to send the producer a letter in which you cite one or more conditions that you find unacceptable: they have been less than candid with you about the thesis of the segment; you feel that the deck is stacked against you; you feel that the editing process is likely to be unfair; they're using sources you believe are prejudiced; they're using stolen, incomplete, or fraudulent documents; you don't believe that your views will be adequately represented; you don't believe that the people preparing the segment really understand the subject matter.

Another way to say no is to allow the other side to do it for you. In your letter, you can say that you're willing to be interviewed if they agree, in writing, to certain conditions: that you'll have the opportunity to get all your points across; that your interview won't be edited; that you'll be able to comment on adverse comments made about you or your organization. While it's most unlikely that they will agree to these conditions, be prepared for the possibility of a positive response – or for further negotiation.

Your third option is to take this last technique one step further, and to force them to say no by requesting conditions they can't possibly accept. These might include unedited airtime without constraints, or allowing you to bring in your own film clips for them to use, or asking them to interview somebody you know they consider unacceptable.

If you decide to say yes, write a straightforward business letter that is neither antagonistic nor adversarial, saying that you are happy to participate in the show, which, you understand, has the following thesis and is going to cover the following points. Specify the areas you're prepared to speak about, but don't mention those you'd prefer to avoid, as that may give them ideas. Specify your understanding of the length of the interview. Reiterate everything your notes show that you were told.

By now the negotiations are over, so don't ask for a response to your letter. In this case, your letter is a unilateral and self-serving document that sets the agenda as you understand it. If the points in your letter prove to be significantly different from the segment, you'll have every reason to complain later.

At this point, you can begin to think about the interview. Let's consider two very different and hypothetical reporters whom we'll call Harry Reasonable and Mike Ambush. No matter who actually interviews you, or even what show they work for, the chances are good that the reporter you speak with will have something in common with either Harry or Mike.

Harry Reasonable is a likeable fellow who may remind you of an older brother or a parish priest. He's the trustworthy, solid, and friendly stranger you might have a conversation with at your neighbourhood bar. His interviewing style is low-keyed, relaxed, and conversational. His goal is to get you to talk while the film runs on and on. If he asks you enough questions, and gives you enough time, he'll eventually get what he wants. With Mike Ambush, as we'll see, you generally know where you stand. But Harry can be tricky. He may induce you to ramble on and say things you shouldn't. When you're dealing with Harry, keep your answers short and don't say too much.

Mike Ambush, on the other hand, is a lot like an assistant district attorney. Mike's looking for the smoking gun, and he goes about it in a face-to-face and confrontational way. He uses a semi-prosecutory style, and he has a special talent for leading his victim into a trap.

Professionally, both Harry and Mike are supremely self-confident. Despite the differences in their technique, they both know what they're looking for and how their going to get there. In order to be effective with either of them, you must match that self-confidence in your interview. And the only way to do that is through proper and rigorous preparation – which we'll get to in a moment.

At the same time, you must accept that no matter how hard you try, and how much you convince yourself that you're their equal, in the final analysis it's they who are in control. If you go into the interview with a macho need to defeat your interviewer, you'll be playing right into their hands.

The object of the game is not to compete with or to beat Mike or Harry. The game is fixed, so that even if you score a few points along the way, those sections probably won't be aired. Keep in mind that *60 Minutes* is one of the most successful television shows in history, which means that CBS – or the network responsible for the programme you're dealing with – will never allow the stars of that show to look bad on the air.

If the object of the game is not to compete with the stars, then what is it? Very simply, this: when the interview finally airs, the audience should think well of you and your views.

Now it's time to prepare for the interview. The most important factor in the interview is your attitude and your confidence, so those are the areas you should work on. Keep in mind that it's your interview, and that you have as many rights as the person who is asking the questions. Don't appear to be intimidated, or you'll be an easy victim. Remind yourself that you have agreed to this interview, and that it could not take place without you. You're not in court; you're here of your own free will.

If you have mountains of material to review, don't read it. It's easy to allow yourself to be inundated with masses of position papers, documents, charts, and memos. This, you may recall, was what happened to President Reagan in the first of his 1984 campaign debates with Walter Mondale. The president was overprepared, and during the debate he became confused. So keep it simple.

If you simply can't resist ploughing through that mountain of papers, then do it only in order to develop the two or three major points you want to make. When you've finished reading everything, put all the papers aside. Take a clean sheet and write down the essential points. Write them again – and again, until they're crisp, clear and colourful.

These are the points you are going to make on the show, and it almost doesn't matter what questions you're asked. Answering their question with your answer is the key to a successful television interview. Of course, this may take some getting used to. To see the masters at work, tune in any Sunday morning and watch as prominent politicians are interviewed on programmes like *Meet the Press* and *Face the Nation*. You'll soon get the hang of it.

While you can't always anticipate the questions, you can – and must – rehearse your answers. A day or two before the show, go through at least two mock interviews, with experts from your own company – and perhaps one or two outsiders – asking you every tough question they can think of. These rehearsals should be done under realistic television conditions, with television lights, cameras, and no interruptions. If you make mistakes during the rehearsal – and you probably will – keep going until the interview is over. Then do it again.

These rehearsals are essential, and it's here that you'll develop the specific terminology and phrasing to be used on the show. When the rehearsals are behind you, you'll know exactly what you're going to say and how you're going to say it. You won't stumble, you won't look bad, and your confidence will soar.

After each of these mock interviews, force yourself to watch them as they're played back. Be ruthless and cold-blooded as you pay close attention not only to what you said, but to how you said it and how you look on the screen. (This will be painful, but do it anyway.) With the help of a colleague, pick out your weak points and work on correcting them during the next rehearsal. You'll be amazed at the improvement.

Warning: Much of the advice that follows is anti-intellectual. It reduces substances to surface trivialities. It pays more attention to the medium than the message. It downplays the importance of important information and intelligent arguments.

Unfortunately, these are the qualities you need to be effective on television. If you are a novice at being interviewed, or if you would like more information, visit a television consultant or pick up a book such as *Mastering the Public Spotlight* by Arnold Zenker.

One of Zenker's best points is that you shouldn't listen to those well-meaning friends and colleagues who urge you to simply 'be yourself' on television. That advice makes sense only if the real you is particularly effective in front of the camera. But what if the real you is so nervous that it undermines your interview? What if the real you talks too much? What if the real you has a tendency to be boring?

Your mission is not to be exactly the same on television as you are at the office. Your mission is to be effective, which may mean that you have to be a bit of an actor on television. People in show business – and *60 Minutes* is show business – are familiar with this dichotomy, which is why they talk of being 'on' when the camera is running. Don't worry about being perceived as phony. Well over 99 per cent of the people watching you at home don't know you from any other context. The others will be impressed by how well you come across.

Another Zenkerism: Always play your comments in the direction of the conversation. Don't be concerned about the viewing audience; a good interview presents the illusion of a discussion on which the listener is simply eavesdropping. Maintain eye contact with the interviewer, and let the director worry about where to position the cameras.

Never forget that television is a visual medium. The person sitting out there is a passive viewer who's going to go away with an impression of you. You might be making a brilliant argument, but what the viewer will remember is whether your necklace jangled every time you turned your head, or whether the shape of your moustache made you look like a shifty character.

On some news shows, like *MacNeil/Lehrer*, a makeup person will be on hand to help you look much better on television than you do in real life. On other shows, including *60 Minutes*, you will be told that makeup isn't necessary. In my view, it always is. If you're going to be on a show that doesn't provide a makeup person, bring your own. It's worth the expense.

Visit your barber or hairdresser a day or two before the interview. On the actual day of the interview, don't go to work. Instead, consider going for a swim or a long walk, having a massage or a facial, taking a nap – or any combination of the above.

Consider bringing some kind of prop to your interview. It may be a chart that you suddenly unroll, or a document that's connected to your story, or some small and relevant piece of equipment that you suddenly produce out of your pocket. If you're able to show something other than your own face, you're providing a point of focus and a little variety for the audience. But understand that your little trick may not survive the editing process.

THE THIRD PERIOD

If you can afford it, bring your own own television crew into the interview. Otherwise, make an audio tape. But it's critical that you have a complete record of the entire interview. For one thing, you might need to use it later if you have serious complaints about the show. For another, the knowledge that you have the interview on tape may serve to keep the producer honest – especially later, during the editing process. And if your film people are in the room, their very presence will have a certain restraining effect on the interviewer.

Because only a small portion of your interview will actually be aired, be prepared to make your main points again and again. Don't worry about repeating yourself. You want to create a situation such that no matter which clip they use, your essential message will be on it.

During the interview, never concede a point unless you fully intend to. Invariably, your concession is what they'll decide to use. Your interview is only as strong as its weakest link.

If you're asked to answer a question that you've previously answered, and you were happy with that answer, you should politely refuse. 'I've already answered that question,' you can say, 'and you have my answer on tape. So why are you asking it again?'

Another request you should politely refuse is that you pose for 'reverse shots' when the interview is over. During the actual interview, the camera will probably be on you the whole time. Later, the producer may want to photograph the interviewer in conversation with you for scenes that will later be spliced in to run with your answers. These shots can be used to make you look bad, which is why you shouldn't do them.

It doesn't happen often, but if something goes terribly wrong during the interview or you feel that you are being taken advantage of, don't rule out the possibility of terminating the conversation in the middle. If that's your decision, be polite and explain what you're doing. Then take off the microphone and calmly walk out of the room. Remember, though, that the camera will still be running as you leave.

When the interview is over, and your memory of it is still fresh, ask yourself whether there were any significant omissions or errors in the questioning. If so, point them out in a letter to the producer.

From this point on, you probably won't hear anything more from the producer of the segment. But if you were interviewed as part of a major documentary, or if the segment you were on is deemed unusually newsworthy, the network may arrange an advance press screening for the critics. This practice irritates me for two reasons. First, because I've been in the ludicrous position of having journalists call me for comments on a show that I'm part of but haven't seen. Second, because this practice of prescreening a 'news' show strips away the veneer of journalistic respectability that television likes to claim for itself. After all, what kind of journalist previews his story to other journalists before it's even published? That's not journalism; it's show business. And if it happens with your segment, consider making a public protest.

Once the show is aired, and if you believe it was unfair, there are several actions you can take. A while back, *60 Minutes* did a show on nuclear power and concentrated on Illinois Power. But the company was prepared: it had brought its own crew to the interview. Because the utility believed that the *60 Minutes* segment was highly biased, Illinois Power made available its own segment, based on the same interview, and distributed it to various groups and corporations.

In such a situation, of course, you have no hope of correcting the record with the general public. But you may be able to reach selected constituencies, such as employees and shareholders. You may cause professional embarrassment to the people who prepared the segment. Finally, your action may lead to favourable press coverage, especially from the print media, who are always eager to criticize their better-paid colleagues who work in television.

You can also respond in less dramatic ways. You can demand that the network investigate its own show and make the results public. (Internal network investigations are fairly common, but they're usually done secretly.) You can issue the corporate equivalent of a white paper – a government-issued document that examines a particular event or situation in exhaustive detail. You can take out a full-page ad to detail the various errors and omissions in the segment. (For examples of this technique, see chapter 3.) You can call a press conference. You can enlist the support of a reporter who is willing to tell your side of the story.

You can also confront network officials and demand that they give you time to respond. They won't, of course, but your demand may have some public-relations value. You can ask the network to sell you time to tell your side of the story. They won't do this, either, but it's still worth trying, as they can't maintain this absurd position forever. Finally, if all else fails, you can consider a libel suit. But this is very tricky, because the only way you can win is by proving malice on their part.

UNDERSTANDING PRINT JOURNALISM

HOW PRINT JOURNALISM DIFFERS FROM TELEVISION
Much of the cautionary advice I have just given about shows like *60 Minutes* does not really apply to print media. Print reporters are less likely to be hostile, in part because they're judged by very different criteria than their peers in television. In general, print stories give you – as a source – the opportunity to be flexible, bold, and constructive in a way that is simply impossible with television.

One major difference is that with print journalism, the person interviewing you will also be writing the story. This means, among other things, that there is a higher chance that your remarks will be reported accurately and in their proper context. (Television journalism, by contrast, is much more of a corporate enterprise.) Among the print media, *Time* and *Newsweek* are exceptions to this rule, as their stories are researched by reporters but written by writers.

At the same time, print journalism presents the possibility of talking to a reporter without being identified in the final story. While that's possible in television, it's much more difficult to arrange.

In the previous chapter, I attacked the widespread use of anonymous quotations, and my personal policy is only to talk on the record. At the same time, you should understand that there are several different ways that you can talk to a reporter:

On the Record. Anything you say can be quoted directly and attributed to you by name. Remember the 'default' assumption: unless you have clearly established otherwise, you are always on the record. Below are the other categories you can use. Keep in mind that you can weave in and out of them during the same conversation.

Off the Record. You're giving the reporter information that he can't use in the story. Unfortunately, 'off the record' does not apply retroactively, so be sure to establish this ground rule before you reveal sensitive information.

Not for Attribution. The reporter can directly quote the information, but he can't ascribe it to you by name. If you're worried about being identified, be sure to negotiate with the reporter about the exact wording of the attribution – 'a knowledgeable insider,' 'a Wall Street analyst,' 'an observer,' and so on.

Background. The reporter can use the information but not quote it, and the attribution must remain general, as in 'according to a company official . . .'

Deep Background. The reporter can use the information but not quote it, and he may not attribute it to anybody. In other words, he must say it on his own, as if he learned it by divine revelation.

Print journalism also allows you special opportunities to be sure that you've been quoted correctly. If you ask in advance, most reporters will agree to call you back to go over – for accuracy – any statements of yours that they might use in the story. If the story involves delicate issues or technical information, you can take this practice a step further. Tell the reporter that you'd prefer to take down his questions and give him your answers in writing. Because you can keep a copy of your statement, there is no need to check quotes. And because you can take your time and answer the questions properly, you won't run the risk of saying something you'll regret.

Another reason I prefer print journalism to television or radio is that you have more time to answer the questions. On an immediate level, you don't have to confine your answer to twenty-five seconds. On a broader scale, you have the luxury of telling the reporter that you'd like to think about his questions. You can suggest that he call you again later in the day, after you've had a chance to consider his questions and, if it's appropriate, to do some research.

Most print stories have a longer lead time than television stories. Important stories may be developed over several weeks, and some magazine pieces can take months. (An article in *The New Yorker* can actually take a year or more, although when it's finally published you may need another six months to finish reading it.) Because he's not under severe time pressure, the reporter on these stories can take the time to understand the issues and get the facts right. He can read through relevant material, and can make use of a research staff. And as the story develops, you can always go back to him with new or updated information.

Print reporters tend to specialize. Whereas business reporters for television news shows are often expected to cover the entire business world, major newspapers and magazines assign a different specialist for each area, such as banking, autos, advertising, the stock market, takeovers, and so forth. As a result, the reporter and the source begin their relationship with a significant and shared expertise, which often makes for a more accurate and sophisticated story.

Another difference between print journalism and television is that with print stories, you don't have to be passive. In TV news interviews, there is enough time to make only one point. As a result, you must be very clear in your mind as to what that point is, and how, exactly, you can best express it in twenty-five seconds.

With reporters from the print media, however, you can be far more flexible. You can give longer answers. You can volunteer new information. You can raise – and respond to – questions that the reporter may not have considered. And if you think that the reporter hasn't really thought through the story, you can offer your own perspective on the larger issue.

Within limits, you can even take issue with the reporter's language and terminology. Not long ago, I was interviewed about my views on political action committees, which I happen to favour. When the reporter talked about 'reforms,' I challenged his use of that word, which implied that PACs were somehow wrong or dirty. I was able to convince him that he should be writing instead about *changes* in the law.

While I much prefer dealing with print journalists than their counterparts in the electronic media, I don't want to romanticize the world of newspapers. Newspapers are a business, after all, and they have to publish every day. 'A newspaper,' observed Henry Fielding in *Tom Jones*, 'consists of just the same number of words, whether there be any news in it or not.' Even on days when there is relatively little to report, newspapers must publish. Advertising never stops, and how else would the publishers of newspapers get their readers to look at those ads if there were no news to surround them?

Newspapers are the mainstay of print journalism, but they are by no means the only players. Those who are outside of the journalistic profession often overlook the importance of the wire services, which include the Associated Press, United Press International, the Dow Jones Service, and Reuters. Most wire service reporters don't enjoy the glamour or name recognition of their colleagues on the *Post* or the *Times* – they are among the few print journalists around whose work appears anonymously – but their access to good sources and critical information is excellent. Their importance is widely recognized by official Washington, which makes sure that the top wire service reporters are routinely assigned the best seats at newsmaking events. And it is a wire service reporter who begins and ends each presidential news conference.

The Associated Press in particular is enormously powerful, if for no other reason than its ability to communicate instantly with media outlets around the country. Hint to potential revolutionaries: If you should ever want to overthrow the federal government without violence or force, simply seize control of the AP ticker for two hours. The rest should be easy.

Then there are the newsweeklies: *Time*, *Newsweek*, and *US News & World Report*. Compared to the daily press, these magazines operate on a more relaxed schedule. Their deadlines are weekly, not daily, which means that they usually have time to go deeper into a story. As a result, you have more time to develop your position with them.

The newsweeklies differ from the daily press in other respects, too. The quality of their research is usually better. Their readership is truly national – and international. They routinely undertake far more research and reporting than they use, so if you're interviewed by *Newsweek*, don't be surprised if your name is never mentioned – or even if the story never runs. Finally, the stories filed by their journalists are heavily edited by the home office. It's only in recent years that these magazines have started to identify the reporters who have worked on individual articles.

On the next level, there are the major opinion magazines. Don't be misled by their relatively small circulation, for these magazines are read by journalists and other opinion makers, and an important story in any of them will be noticed. *The Atlantic*, published in Boston, was a sleepy old monthly until it published the famous interview with David Stockman. More recently, its articles on defence by James Fallows have been required reading. *Commentary* has a circulation of under 50,000, but its influence in neoconservative circles can scarcely be overstated.

Other opinion magazines and newspapers include *The*

National Review and *The Public Interest*, on the right; *The Nation, Mother Jones, Rolling Stone*, and the *Village Voice*, on the left; and *The New Yorker, Harper's* and *The New Republic*, somewhere in the middle.

WHEN THE PRESS COMES TO YOU

Often, when reporters approach you for an interview, they will imply that you have no real choice in the matter. They may say or suggest that if you don't cooperate, you'll be violating some unwritten law, or that your noncooperation will make you look bad. Don't fall for any of this. Always talk to the press because you want to, or because it will be good for you or your institution. But never do so because you have to.

Don't let a journalist intimidate you into talking to him by telling you that it's in your interest to cooperate. He could be right, but that decision should be yours, not his. And watch out for the reporter who argues that you might as well talk to him because he's going to do the story anyway. That's not always the case. It may be that without your help there won't be a story. So feel free to ask the reporter whom else he's going to interview, and what his sources are, and make your own decision.

Sometimes, if you are reluctant to answer a reporter's questions, he will insist that the public has the right to know these things. If that happens, you might remind him that while the public is entitled to know certain information, that data is transmitted by your company to the appropriate government agencies. You might also remind the reporter that it is not your practice to share confidential or proprietary information with representatives of another business – especially if that other business depends upon the selling of such information.

By the same token, don't allow reporters to seduce you. This can be done in any number of ways, but flattery is high on the list, as is the technique of making the source feel that he's central to the story. Some people, when confronted with a reporter, start to lose their common sense. Once, during a difficult interview for *60 Minutes*, Mike Wallace said to his subject, with the cameras running and the lights on, 'Just between you and me, can you tell me what *really* happened?' The ploy worked like a charm.

There are other common methods of seduction. 'I'm your

friend,' says the reporter warmly. 'You can trust me. Just be open with me and tell me everything.'

This is an appealing and seductive approach, especially when it's made to people who are afraid of the press. But don't be taken in. While the reporters who say these things are often completely sincere, they can afford to be. But you can't.

Very often, the press is your adversary. In many cases, and perhaps most, the aim of the reporter is to encourage you to say things that you shouldn't say. Naturally, one way to accomplish this is to provide a warm and friendly environment that will lead you to drop your guard and say things you'll soon regret.

Keep in mind that the press is never really off duty. Even though you may be talking to a reporter in a social setting or a cocktail party, don't assume that your conversation is confidential or off the record. If they're forced to choose, most reporters probably won't – and shouldn't – allow friendship to interfere with a good story.

Unless you have an explicit agreement with the reporter that what you're saying at that moment is off the record, anything you tell the press at any time is grist for the mill. So if you don't want the information to be made public, don't discuss it with a reporter.

I learned my lesson a few years ago. One fine spring day I strolled over to a nearby park to eat my lunch. I sat down on a bench, where I soon found myself in discussion with a fellow eater, who turned out to be reporter. The next day, I read about our conversation in the paper. Fortunately, no harm was done, but it was a mistake I'll never repeat.

Other journalists will take a very different approach. They may try to convince you that they're morally or intellectually superior to you, or that they represent the public more than you do. These are the techniques of intimidation, and you must not surrender to them. Your objective is to put yourself on an equal footing with the journalist, and, if he insists on a confrontation (and he probably won't), to make clear that you're tougher and better informed than he is.

Remember, you are the expert. The reporter is asking the questions, and you're helping him by providing the answers so that he can write his story. If you don't like his questions, or even the way that he's asking them, you don't have to cooperate. You are never obliged to speak to the press, or to give reporters documents or information, or to let them decide what's right or wrong. You may choose to cooperate with members of the press, but that should always be your decision and not theirs.

There will be times when you will decide not to say anything to a reporter. In these situations, try to avoid saying 'no comment.' Some reporters see that phrase as a slap in the face, while to others it's merely an evasive statement by which you hint broadly that all of the bad things they're thinking about you are true.

Does this mean that you should always answer any question? Of course not! You can legitimately have no comment; it's just that you shouldn't use those particular words. Sometimes you can defuse the situation with humour, as in 'Come on, now, you've got to be kidding!' Or: 'You don't really expect me to answer that question, do you?' Or even: 'Listen, I really like my job . . .'

Another way of avoiding comment is to say something colourful that sounds like an answer but is essentially meaningless. The press wants substance, but when it can't get substance, it will settle for colour. Hubie Brown, coach of the New York Knicks, is a master at this technique. Several years ago, when the Knicks where in the midst of a particularly bad losing streak, a reporter approached Brown and asked, 'Do you contemplate any changes in your lineup?'

'Well,' responded Hubie with a wise expression on his face, 'we'll have to see how the bagels taste tomorrow.'

Here are some other alternatives to 'no comment':

- I won't even accept the question.
- That question is unanswerable.
- The premise behind your question is so erroneous that I can't possibly give you an answer.
- To answer that question I'd have to do all your research for you.

MAINTAINING AN ONGOING RELATIONSHIP WITH THE PRESS

QUESTION: How many public-relations people does it take to change a light bulb?
ANSWER: Gee, I don't know. Can I get back to you later?

Passive press relations may be as bad as having no press relations at all. (Come to think of it, it may be worse. Charles de Gaulle,

Frank Sinatra, and countless professional athletes have turned their disdain for the press into a genuine asset.) Most institutions wait for a crisis – and even then they're rarely prepared to deal with reporters. Don't wait for an emergency. The time to initiate contact with the press is now – when there's no story to report.

You should meet the press more than halfway by arranging tours, interviews with top management, and out-of-the-office contacts. Nobody every bought an editor for the price of a lunch, but it can't hurt to establish a relationship in advance so that there's a human face – yours – in the editor's memory when the story develops. If you've worked on these contacts, the press may ask for your comment even when your institution isn't directly involved in the story, which will certainly enhance both your credibility and that of your corporation.

To avoid misunderstanding, let me be explicit: I am not talking here about cozying up to the press, or even being friends with reporters. But you can't build communication and understanding with people you see only in adversarial situations.

Another reason to stay in touch with reporters is that they can teach you a great deal. Very often, in fact, reporters can be your best source of information. In the news business, as in Washington, information is currency. If you build a good relationship with a reporter, you may find that you'll learn as much from him as he'll learn from you. Remember, reporters speak to everybody. I'm not suggesting that journalists can – or will – spy on your opponents or competitors. But when you talk with somebody who's well informed, not all of the information flows in the same direction. And even if the reporter is discreet, you can often learn something simply by paying attention to his questions.

At the same time, you will often have information that you don't want the press to know about. Here's a little trick: If there's something you want to hide, but are required to disclose, put it in a press release. One casualty of 'investigative reporting' is that most journalists find it hard to take seriously what you give them willingly. What they value is what they learn on their own, or from other people. The sceptical reporter won't even look at a press release, which is why you might want to use that vehicle for material that you must reveal but don't want to call attention to.

If your objective is to advance a point of view, one option is to seek a meeting with the editorial board of a major newspaper. These people are not reporters; they're the faceless committee of intelligent and well-informed writers who turn out the daily editorials. Generally, the members of the editorial board are each responsible for several different topics, and they come to their positions through discussions with their colleagues. Because editorial writers tend to be insulated, they're often eager to sit down and talk with people who have information and insights on important issues of public policy.

The atmosphere of these meetings is that of a seminar. You're not there to lecture, but to articulate your point of view and to participate in the discussion. Sometimes the meeting is held so that the editorial board can get to know an authority in a particular field, who shares his views on a wide range of topics. At other times the meeting takes place around a particular issue. In other cases, you should assume that similar meetings have been scheduled with people representing other points of view.

Large newspapers will often turn the event into a luncheon and will invite some of their reporters as well. Assume that everything you say in such a setting will be on the record. With smaller papers, a visit with the editor of the editorial page is generally sufficient to get your views across.

It is perfectly acceptable to seek such a meeting on your own: you simply write to the editor of the editorial page and say that you would like the opportunity to meet with the board on a particular date.

Incidentally, this is one area in which public-relations people should be careful. It's preferable that the person making the request be the individual with hands-on responsiblity or the top person of the organization.

In the event that you have any doubts on this point, consider the famous 1982 memo from Meg Greenfield, editor of the *Washington Post*'s editorial page, to the paper's executive editor and managing editor. Shortly after having been contacted by a PR firm to set up a lunch with a senator whom she had known for years, Ms Greenfield proclaimed that all public-relations firms were to be banned from her realm. Somebody at the *Post* copied the memo and sent a copy to every PR firm in town.

'We have adopted a rule of simply refusing to deal with these people – period. I have myself told some slave or other from Hill & Knowlton that we don't traffic with press agents, that if her client, a college president, had business to transact with us, then the college president should call.' Greenfield continued: 'If people want to get to us, they need to know only [that it's] as easy as pie so long as they don't come in (or send their manuscripts in or make their request) via a flack firm.'

The resentment on the part of the press towards public-relations firms is broad-based and complex, but one element of it has to do with the fact that the press believes that public-relations people are concerned only with hiding the warts of their clients, rather than disseminating useful informating. A more subtle element of this animosity may be that corporate PR people generally make a lot more money than their counterparts who work for newspapers.

At any rate, another way to get your story, or your view, reported in the press is to seek a meeting with a columnist or a reporter. You can contact members of this group by sending them a letter together with some appropriate literature. You can also call them; all journalists are open to approach. But pick your target carefully: you're far better off choosing a columnist with some ideological or personal interest in your cause.

In general, the best way to catch the attention of a reporter is to provide him with information, especially information that deals with some kind of dissention or strife. Remember: reporters love to write about conflict and disagreement. You can't get away with a press release, you'll have to provide documented information that disputes or disagrees with something someone else has said. It's even better if you can provide documented evidence of a high-level ideological conflict.

In general, the first approach to the press is the most difficult. With reporters, as with everybody else, success begets more success, as people like to be associated with a winner. Assuming that you've received some favourable publicity for your cause in newspaper articles and editorials, make a package of them and send it around to selected reporters.

Or, if you prefer, you can go further by putting together a press kit on your cause or issue, consisting not only of clippings, but also any other relevant material that will help the reader understand the issue and appreciate your point of view. Be sure to include any interviews you or your group has done, as well as your own question-and-answer pieces. Send the press kits to decision makers as well as reporters. Remember: your purpose is to educate the reader about your issue, so start from the beginning and don't assume anything.

Making an approach to the press does not mean, of course, that you should try to seduce the press. Some people, perhaps because they're intimidated by the news media, view reporters as a macho challenge to be overcome through the force of their personality. If you play that game, you'll probably lose.

Treat reporters as you would want to be treated. Don't try to dazzle them with food and drink, and don't offer them gifts. These tactics will not only fail, they will backfire and lead reporters to turn against you.

Don't try to make friends with reporters, but do try to establish a real relationship. If a reporter gets to know you, he can respond to you as an individual instead of as the representative of an institution.

Finally, there will be times when all of this advice will still not be enough, and you suddenly find yourself in a situation in which the press has treated you unfairly. If that ever happens, be sure to complain. Most reporters try to be fair, and want to see themselves as objective. If you honestly think a story is biased against you, let the reporter and his editor know. Make your points in a cool and rational way, and provide evidence for your contention. When the *Wall Street Journal* repeatedly attacked Chrysler during that company's brush with bankruptcy, Lee Iacocca met with the editors and showed them a scrapbook of anti-Chrysler clippings. Thereafter, the stories about Chrysler were more balanced.

Once when Mobil was treated unfairly in a newspaper story, we made a big blowup of the article, mounted in on pasteboard, circled the errors, and corrected them in the margins. Then we gift-wrapped the package and sent it to the reporter. I think we made our point, although on other occasions, when the errors were less serious, we have responded in quieter and more conventional ways.

In the fall of 1984, I was troubled by a story in the *Washington Post* whose headline read: 'Former Mobil Consultant Sentenced in Bribery Case.' The man, who had indeed once worked for Mobil, had been convicted of a crime that had nothing to do with his work for us. After reading the story, I sent a handwritten letter to Ben Bradlee, the executive editor, in which I asked: 'How would you feel if the headline read "*Washington Post* Subscriber Convicted of Bribery"? Such a headline would make as much sense as the one in the enclosed article. I've never seen our employees so upset over an article.'

Bradlee answered my letter: 'I guess I'd be pissed,' he replied.

'But wouldn't "*Washington Post* Subscriber" be more properly equated with 'Mobil Gas User'? Anyway, it was a reach and a totally inappropriate reach, and I'm sorry for it.'

Reporters and editors are understandably sensitive about mistakes, so it's always best to make your complaint with a cheerful feistiness, and to point out their errors with a little wit rather than a heavy-handed or bombastic attack.

In sum, then, your successful relationship with the members of the press depends upon how realistic you are. If you don't romanticize their objectives, if you recognize that they're usually not terribly well versed in the nuances of business, and if you're willing to be confrontational to the extent that it's necessary, then you have an excellent chance of achieving your objectives. In the next chapter, we'll look in detail at one of those objectives – reaching the opinion makers.

SIX

Reaching the Opinion Makers

People in our society often talk about an idea whose time has come. But life is rarely that simple, and new ideas don't just suddenly appear on the scene as if by divine revelation. More often than not, the development and acceptability of an idea is a subtle, layered process – something like throwing a stone into a still pond and watching the ripples move out.

Most new ideas gain currency and acceptability because they are discussed by people who are regarded as important. I hesitate to use the term *opinion maker* here, because that term has been overworked and its currency cheapened by Madison Avenue. But the fact remains that certain people in our society are seen as creators or arbiters of public policy. Some have attained that rank because of the positions they hold in government, religion, business, or education. Another group consists of members of the news media. Others are listened to because of their intellectual or academic credentials, such as teachers, professors, and researchers. Still others are active in consumer or environmental groups, or in show business. Finally, there are those who are listened to because they are prominent. 'In every town in Texas,' LBJ once remarked, 'there's a guy who lives in a big white house on a hill. These are the guys I want with me.'

No corporation, no matter what its resources, is likely to change public opinion. Your actual purpose here is far more modest: to inject yourself into the debate, and to make sure your viewpoint is heard by the intellectual establishment. Whether anybody actually pays attention depends on the quality of the ideas – and the way they are presented.

There are several ways to achieve this. One is to make sure that you (or, if you're a public-relations professional, your top management) are knowledgeable on the key issues and able to articulate your views in meetings, in interviews, and during social occasions. Another is to be sure that your voice (or, again, the voice of your leadership) is heard directly through bylined articles in newspapers and magazines, and even letters to the editor. A third way is through public speeches and debates, especially if they are reported in the press.

We at Mobil have specialized in a fourth way – issue advertising – which I will be discussing here in some detail. But no matter which route you take, the principle is the same: you have to express yourself as clearly and as intelligently as possible. If you're unable to present a convincing argument based on hard data and sound philosophy, you will fail.

At the same time, what you say is only as effective as how you say it. Don't be a complainer, because the public doesn't respond to a company what whines or carps. But people admire a fighter, and they respect an organization that sticks its neck out when it considers itself to be in the right. Whether it's an op-ed article, a letter to the editor, or an issue ad of the sort I'll be discussing here, make your prose feisty, without being disagreeable, and you'll find an audience who will pay attention to your arguments.

I'm going to dwell at some length on the Mobil op-ed ad program because it has been unusually successful. In political terms, the ads constitute the platform on which we run. Each week, in effect, we add another plank or reinforce a previous one. To continue the analogy, we are continually seeking new supporters among the undecided, and one way we do this is by a continuing series of position papers on the important issues of the day.

We at Mobil are proud of our op-ed programme, but we are by no means its only admirers. We are continually hearing from authors, publishers, and colleges who want to reprint our ads in textbooks, and from graduate students who want to write about them in dissertations.

Several years ago, a study by the International Advertising Association concluded that the Mobil programme is 'the single most significant campaign of this nature ever undertaken, regardless of country.' And Milton Moskowitz, a columnist who is known for his criticisms of big business, has given us the ultimate compliment. 'Most corporate advertising,' he says, 'is still only flatulent rhetoric. Most companies are just talking to each other to make their directors feel good. But I'm in favour of what Mobil is doing. They are more aggressive than most of the others and far more effective. They get under your skin, which is the way to start a real dialogue.'

In 1970, when our op-ed programme began in the *New York Times*, there were at least three major issues facing the oil industry. First, we at Mobil were concerned that in the relatively near future, America and the rest of the free world would be vulnerable to politically motivated oil cutoffs from foreign governments. Owing to a rapidly depleting supply of domestic crude oil, the United States was becoming increasingly reliant of foreign sources of energy. As we saw it, this fundamental change in America's energy supply was bound to have significant and possibly even dangerous effects on the political, social, and economic fabric of our nation.

Back in 1970, however, the prospect of an energy shortage was just about the last thing on people's minds. The economy was prosperous in the land of plenty, and anyone who foresaw a different scenario was regarded as a latter-day Chicken Little. Still, we were concerned about the future. We argued strongly for action that would lead to a greater supply of domestic energy, including the deregulation of natural gas and oil prices, the opening up of offshore drilling opportunities, increased nuclear power, and a more balanced and realistic policy of environmental legislation.

This last issue – the environment – was our second major concern. The 1960s had seen the emergence of a powerful environmental lobby, partly because the environment served as the perfect 'motherhood' issue for a good many politicians and journalists. Everybody was in favour of clean air and clean water, which made it conveniently easy to vilify those who expressed any reservations as to the goals or methods of the new movement.

But those who served in the management positions of large industrial corporations knew full well that perfectly clean air and perfectly clean water could not be achieved without spending truly staggering sums of money. We were the ones who had to worry about the cost of these programmes. Of course we favoured a clean environment; who wouldn't? But it was clear to us that there would have to be some trade-offs between what was ideal and what was realistic. At the time, this was a message that few people wanted to hear.

The third issue that concerned us was that American business institutions were under fire as never before. As a number of polls had made all too clear, big business in general and the oil industry in particular had suffered a significant erosion in public confidence. In some circles, these antibusiness feelings were widened to include a deep scepticism about our entire free-market economic system.

In the face of these growing attacks on business, we knew we had to make a significant response. Although most other corporations were silent, the ostrichlike response just wasn't our style. Starting with Rawleigh Warner, Jr., our new chairman, the management of Mobil was eager to participate in the national dialogue. We were ready to speak out on a host of economic and political issues. The only question was how.

At around the same time, editors at the *New York Times* had just decided on a major change in the paper's editorial page. In an effort to open up the paper and to feature diverse opinions and commentaries by both staff columnists and guest writers, the *Times* instituted what soon came to be called the op-ed page – that is, a second editorial page opposite the original one. The management of the *Times* decided to devote a quarter of this new page to advertising – at a small premium over the regular rates.

The kind of advertising that the *Times* had in mind for its second editorial page would not be designed to sell goods and services. Its purpose, rather, was to allow corporations to enhance and polish their identity. This is traditionally referred to as 'image advertising,' a technique that occasionally leads me to suspect that the company in question is spending more money to publicize their good deeds than they spend on the deeds themselves. Image advertising is always warm and never controversial. Its objective is to tell the reader how great your company is, and its motivation, in a phrase, is to get people to love you.

For us at Mobil, however, the advertising space on the op-ed page represented a very different kind of opportunity. Here was an ideal chance to speak our mind to opinion makers! In using that term, I don't mean that we had in mind a small elite. While from time to time our ads might be directed towards one person – the president of the United States, for example – or towards a small group – say, the members of a congressional committee – for the most part we wanted to reach anyone who would expend the time and effort to read our messages. In other words, if you cared enough to read our point of view, you were enough of an activist for our purposes, and we were delighted that ours was one of the viewpoints that you were being exposed to.

Although there was no line for this kind of advertising in our public-affairs budget, we quickly signed up for a series of thirteen ads on the op-ed page.

Now that we had made a commitment, it was time to formulate some basic decisions regarding the nature of our ads. One thing that was clear from the start was that, unlike our product advertising, these issue ads – or advertorials, as they came to be known in the press – had to be written in-house. When you're dealing with important issues of public policy, its unfair to expect that your ad agency can understand your business and your thinking well enough to express your views on the issues of the day. Moreover, the timeliness of the ads and the necessity of having them cleared by top management required that the turnaround process be as fast as possible.

We also decided to make the ads fairly substantial. Instead of seeing our messages in terms of conventional advertising, the model we had in mind was the thoughtful newspaper editorial. This might mean, on occasion, that our messages would be fairly long and complex. But we felt that the public had a right to know more than our conclusion. We decided to show the intellectual basis for our arguments, so that the reader would be aware of the various assumptions we hold and the philosophy that influences our views.

At the same time, we certainly didn't want to be ponderous. And so we attempted to develop a crisp style that would convey a well-supported viewpoint to a sophisticated audience without boring the reader.

Another critical ingredient was accuracy. Because our programme was bound to be controversial, we realized that we just couldn't afford to make any errors. Our credibility was on the line, which meant that even a minor mistake could destroy months of good work. So from the start, it was clear that our research would be as important as our writing.

When it came to matters of tone and style, we wanted to take the offensive without being offensive. Our messages would be urbane and, when possible, good-humoured; they would not be pompous or bland. They would comment on issues, but they would also show other facets of our corporate personality by celebrating good works and excoriating ineptitude. Our ads would also, on occasion, serve to wheedle, cajole, josh, and admonish our readers.

Finally, there was the question of how the ads would look. I remember insisting that those messages that dealt directly with issues of substance should contain no illustrations. Although my view prevailed, the decision was far from unanimous.

The other aesthetic considerations were arrived at more easily. It was clear that the ads would have to fit in with Mobil's distinctive graphic style. At the same time, they would also have to be suitably integrated into the two-page editorial spread in the *Times*. It sounded easy enough, but this turned out to be a fairly tricky proposition. If our ads were too similar to the other columns on the page, they would run the risk of getting lost in the crowd. If they were too different, they would end up fighting with the rest of the paper. Eventually we arrived at a suitable compromise.

Even before the first ad appeared, we understood that this project carried with it certain risks. We knew, for example, that our speaking out in the *Times* would inevitably serve to invigorate our opponents. And it didn't take a genius to realize that our approach would quickly activate that well-entrenched coalition of politicians and self-appointed public guardians who opposed the oil industry on principle, and who would not hesitate to single out Mobil for rebuttal and attack.

We were also aware that it might take many months before our ads yielded any real results. For this reason, we committed ourselves to the long run. We decided that if our project lacked continuity, it was probably not worth doing in the first place.

Despite all of our worries and cautions, we were genuinely excited about this new opportunity. We saw ourselves as practising the ancient and honourable art of pamphleteering—only instead of distributing our tracts from door to door, we found it more economical to pay the *Times* to serve as our delivery system.

Our first op-ed ad appeared on October 19, 1970. 'America has the world's best highways and the world's worst mass transit' read the headline. 'We hope this ad moves people.' Although Mobil's economic health has always been tied closely to the continuing use of private automobiles, we were convinced, especially in view of the possibility of an oil shortage, that the United States urgently needed more and better mass transit.

To our delight, this first ad generated a great deal of attention. Many readers paid attention simply because the position we took seemed to be at odds with our basic economic interest. Certainly this was the first time that a major oil company had come out publicly for improved public transportation. By questioning the

America has the world's best highways And the world's worst mass transit.

We hope this ad moves people...

In recent years the United States has developed a really superb highway system. It's been built with tax revenues earmarked specifically for road building.

But the highway construction boom has been accompanied by a mass transit bust. Train and bus travel in this country, with few exceptions, is decrepit. The air traveler suffers increasing indignities despite bigger, faster planes.

Greater New York is a typical example. You can depend on commuting to and from Manhattan—but only to be undependable and slow. On public transport, the 25 miles to Westfield, N.J. takes 75 minutes at an average speed of 20 miles per hour. The 33 miles to Stamford, Conn. takes 60 minutes at 33 mph. The 26 miles to Hicksville, L.I. takes 55 minutes at 28 mph. When you're on time.

You have to be a stoic with stamina to use public ground transportation for a trip beyond the commuting range. Fly to a nearby city? You can hardly get at our congested air terminals, either by land or air. The ride to or from the airport often takes longer than the flight.

Mass transit seems to work better abroad. Americans are agreeably impressed by the fast, comfortable, and attractive subways in foreign cities. Intercity trains in other countries make ours look pitiful. Japan's high-speed Tokaido line carries more than 200,000 passengers a day. Clean, comfortable French, German, Italian, and British trains regularly attain speeds over 100 mph. European railroads are already planning or building expresses that will do better than 150 mph.

Yet, in the United States, new mass transit systems are for the most part still in the wild blue yonder.

Providing for our future transportation needs will require very large expenditures. We believe there's an urgent need for legislators to reexamine the procedures used to generate and expend transportation revenues. Such a review may yield the conclusion that special earmarked funds are no longer the best approach.

In weighing priorities, no decision-maker can ignore the increasing congestion on those fine highways of ours, especially in and around the great urban centers. But more and better mass transit could stop traffic jams before they start. Just one rail line has triple the people-moving capacity of a three-lane superhighway.

It costs less—in energy consumption and in money—to move people via mass transit than on highways. Thus mass transit means less air pollution.

It also means conservation. Whether the energy comes from gasoline for cars, or fuel oil, natural gas, or coal for electric power plants, it's derived from a diminishing natural resource. So we think *all* forms of transportation should be brought into a national plan for safe, rapid, economical ways of moving people—consistent with the wisest use of our energy resources.

While Mobil sells fuels and lubricants, we don't believe the gasoline consumed by a car idling in a traffic jam (carrying a single passenger, probably) is the best possible use of America's limited petroleum resources. Our products ought to help more people get where they want to go.

To us, that means a green light for mass transit . . . soon.

Mobil

wisdom of continuing to build expensive highways, we infuriated several constituencies that had traditionally been our allies, including the heavy-equipment industry, the construction industry, and, most of all, the other major oil companies. These groups saw our advocacy of mass transit as a betrayal, and they didn't hesitate to let us know of their disappointment.

On the other side, many of our long time critics were also caught off guard, because with this one ad we were undermining the convenient monolithic image of the industry that everybody loved to hate. Some of our liberal critics smelled a plot and waited for the other shoe to drop. They're still waiting.

By the time our thirteen ads ran, it was already clear that our messages had been noticed, read, discussed, and reprinted. During the following months, we continued to buy space in the *Times* on an ad hoc basis. Finally, after a year or two had gone by, Rawleigh Warner called me one day and asked, 'Why don't we do this every week?'

'Maybe we should,' I replied, 'but I don't know whether we can sustain it. Let me see if we can get a dozen ads into the hopper.' We did, so I went back to Warner and we agreed to continue the project on a weekly basis. We have been doing it ever since.

The *Times* has never interferred with our op-ed ads, even when we have directly taken issue with their editorials. There was only one case of censorship, and it was more amusing than disturbing. Early in 1971, Mayor John Lindsay and eleven thousand sanitation workers found something they could agree on: plastic garbage bags. The mayor signed into law a bill allowing New Yorkers to use approved garbage bags instead of the old metal cans. This was a programme that we at Mobil were eager to support – first, because it made urban living just a little more pleasant, and second, because we ourselves were in the plastic-garbage-bag business.

Now it was clear to just about every New York resident that one of the biggest garbage problems in the city concerned Monday's disposal of the Sunday *New York Times*. To deal with this problem, and to encourage the use of plastic garbage bags, we developed an ad whose headline read 'All the News That's Fit to Print Today Is Trash Tomorrow.'

Apparently we went too far. While the *Times* had no objection to the content of our ad, they asked us to change the headline because it spoofed their corporate slogan. It was a reasonable request, and we changed the headline to the rather more prosaic 'Neat News for Waste Watchers.' Fortunately, this one incident has constituted the extent of our problems with the *Times* over our programme. In view of our repeated and unsuccessful attempts to present similar ads on television, we've always been very appreciative of that fact.

For the first couple of years, the ads were done catch-as-catch-can, with writers being assigned on an ad hoc basis. Jack Tolbert, a talented veteran writer who was manager of our public-relations department, wrote most of the early ones. Over time, we started bringing in other writers. In the early years, the writer was responsible for his own research; more recently, those two functions have become separated.

It's not surprising that our greatest challenge over the years has been to maintain our original spirit of sponteneity. While that task has grown increasingly difficult, even today our ads are rarely prepared more than two or three days before publication.

Over the years, Mobil's op-ed ads have dealt with a wide variety of issues. During the two oil crises of the 1970s, for example, we needed to dispel the widespread impression that the oil industry was to blame, or that the oil companies were reaping unconscionable profits. In the wake of the oil crises, we have continually urged the government to adopt a workable energy policy and to let us step up the search for oil. And we have spoken out strongly against legislation that would tear apart the large oil companies.

Another of our major themes has been that everything in life is a trade-off. For example, it is certainly possible for our society to enjoy natural gas at artificially depressed prices. But if that's the choice we make, nobody can guarantee that there will be adequate and secure supplies.

Or to take another example, while it is possible to reduce automotive air emissions severely and abruptly in order to meet an arbitrary timetable, this programme would make it impossible to also hold down costs and improve mileage. In short, we have tried to help people understand what options are open to them and what costs are involved in the various alternatives – matters that few politicians or journalists ever seem to talk about.

In 1974, we published a series of eleven ads in several dozen newspapers across the country, under the umbrella headline 'Towards a National Energy Policy.' This was the most comprehensive project of this kind that we had ever undertaken.

The ads were long and fairly complex. But when we offered free reprints of all of the ads, assembled in an attractive little booklet, more than 11,000 people wrote in, requesting over 25,000 copies of the booklet.

Many of these people were college professors. Many others were in government. We also sent copies to every member of Congress, every cabinet member, and to other members of the administration. In addition, we sent copies to 3,000 media people across the country, to about 10,000 educators, and to some 12,000 high-school libraries. This large-scale secondary distribution was our primary goal when we decided to prepare and publish the series.

When you're selling ideas, the results are especially hard to quantify. But it's clear that through our op-ed ads, we've managed to bring some of our views into the public consciousness. We have won a certain degree of credibility with various key publics, and have apparently convinced at least some of them that the oil industry is neither monolithic nor antediluvian.

In 1976, the Harris organization conducted a poll to learn how the American public viewed forty major corporations, including seven oil companies. Although the oil companies in general fared very poorly, the people surveyed thought more highly of Mobil than of the competition. In their view, Mobil was 'committed to free enterprise,' 'seriously concerned about the energy problems,' and 'working for good government.' In fact, the public perceived Mobil as the industry pacesetter on nineteen of the twenty-one public-policy issues that were mentioned in the survey. Obviously, our op-ed programme was a major factor in our favour.

Moreover, although we had not done any product advertising for nearly three years, the public rated the quality of our products and services higher than the other oil companies and equal to the average of the forty companies in the survey. I think that's evidence that while we may be selling ideas, there are also some bottom-line benefits from our public-affairs programme.

While it would be presumptuous to suggest that our editorial messages have actually made the difference in the public's changing attitudes on certain controversial issues affecting energy and the economy, it does seem that some opinion leaders have been influenced by the arguments we have made. For example, we've spoken out frequently on excessive government regulation. By now, most Americans agree that the federal government has gone too far in its efforts to control American business, and that all of this well-intentioned meddling carries a stiff price tag.

Similarly, we've had our say on the folly of price controls, a mistake that has become increasingly clear now that most controls on oil have been lifted. We've been equally outspoken on the need for a balance between jobs and growth, on the one hand, and a clean environment, on the other. By now, it seems, a majority of the public recognizes the need for sensible trade-offs. And it is interesting to note that jobs and economic growth were prominent issues in the 1984 presidential campaign.

In cases where our views have not prevailed, or where they prevailed only in part, we have at least played a respected role in the debate and received a fair hearing. For a corporation, this is what makes advocacy advertising worth doing.

Over the years, we've also had a lot to say about the role of business in American life. On a number of occasions we've used our space to explain and defend America's economic system, which has been so little understood by our own citizens. We have supported efforts to reduce the federal deficit, and we've paid particular attention to private-sector reports on how the federal government can cut spending. Finally, we have been outspoken about the media's negative treatment of big business.

In addition to whatever intellectual effect our ads have had on the general public, our op-ed programme has also produced several important fringe benefits among certain sub-publics. For one thing, our ads have had a salutory effect on our recruitment programme. For another, there has been a parallel improvement in employee morale, especially among our executives, who have been delighted to see the company standing up for what we think is right. Many of them tell us that they are proud to be associated with an institution that doesn't cut and run when the bullets start to fly.

A third benefit of our op-ed programme is its positive effect on shareholders. When we survey new shareholders, the second-most-prominent reason they give for buying our stock is their belief that Mobil will be active in protecting their investment from hostile government intervention and legislation. If we ever found ourselves in a proxy fight, I'd like to think that this perception on the part of investors would be a significant asset on the side of management.

When it was clear that the ads in the *Times* were reaching their intended audience, we started to run them in other papers as well – the *Los Angeles Times*, the *Chicago Tribune*, the *Boston Globe*, the *Wall Street Journal*, and the *Washington Post*. At one point, during the 1973–74 energy crisis, we were running our op-ed ads in a hundred different newspapers. But that was an unusual situation, and in normal times we've limited ourselves to half a dozen major dailies.

In 1974 we reviewed our op-ed programme and concluded that we had put too strict a definition on who, exactly, constituted an opinion leader. While our messages were certainly reaching a good number of opinion makers, we were ignoring other important sectors of the population. Owing to the nature of our political system, people living in the heartland are often more influential in political terms than the eastern intellectuals. A fuel-oil distributor in Ohio, for example, or the woman who runs a feed mill in Missouri may have a closer personal relationship with their respective congressman than the editor of a big-city newspaper has with his. Many congressional districts lie outside major population areas, and we were especially eager to reach these areas.

So in 1974 we embarked on a magazine campaign aimed at heartland-community readers. Our ads began appearing in places like *Time* and *Reader's Digest*, and in such service-club magazines as *Rotarian*, *Kiwanian*, *Moose*, and *Elks*.

A few months after this campaign was started, I was invited to lunch by an ad agency that did corporate work for a large multinational client. The ad people were interested in stepping up their client's issue advertising, but they complained that Mobil's programme of issue ads had preempted the field to the point that there was nothing left to do. I was flattered, but I strongly disagreed with their conclusion. Preempted the field? That couldn't be. I was convinced that there was plenty of room for a new concept in issue advertising, and I took it as a personal challenge to come up with one.

A few weeks earlier, I had been approached by an old college friend who was now the head of advertising for *Parade*, the Sunday-newspaper-supplement magazine. It was his view that we ought to be running our issue ads in his publication. While I agreed that *Parade* was a good way to reach an entirely different group of readers, I just couldn't see running our ads there. The ads were appropriate in the *Times*, but in *Parade* the environment was all wrong.

Then I hit upon an intriguing idea. What if we designed a different kind of ad, one that was more in keeping with *Parade*'s format? Over a couple of weeks we came up with the idea of a series of short takes that would look something like a gossip column. The new ads would deal with the same themes as our op-ed ads, but they would do so more breezily and informally.

We called the column 'Observations,' and for years we ran it in *Parade, Family Weekly*, and similar Sunday supplements. At its peak, 'Observations' reached approximately half of the households in America through five hundred different newspapers. Later, owing to budget considerations, 'Observations' was put on a monthly schedule and moved to *Reader's Digest*. But I'm convinced that *Parade* represents an unusually good media buy, and I've never regretted advertising there. If our budget allowed it, 'Observations' would still appear in *Parade* every week. But for advertising that appears only once a month, *Reader's Digest* was more appropriate.

While it's always difficult to measure the impact of advertising, the effects of 'Observations' were truly impressive. The readership scores in *Parade* for that column routinely exceeded by a large margin the average scores for other half-page black-and-white ads. Often, 'Observations' did much better than big, four-colour ads and occasionally even outran the editorial columns of the magazine.

We once commissioned a survey to determine whether 'Observations' was really influencing people on public-policy issues that we saw as important. We asked newspaper readers in three cities (Hartford, Conn.; Davenport, Iowa; and Charlotte, N.C.) for their views on seven provocative issues that we had treated frequently in 'Observations.' Then we compared their views with those of newspaper readers in three demographically similar cities (Providence. R.I.; Des Moines, Iowa; and Memphis, Tenn.) where 'Observations' was not seen.

The poll results, based on fairly large samplings, showed significant differences between the two groups on a variety of issues, including nuclear power, limiting the government's role in business, and scepticism about solar energy.

We have always received a great deal of mail from 'Observations' readers. Whether or not they agreed with us, most of our readers supported our right to express our views, and they took time to write to us. Many of them pointed out the vital role that 'Observations' played in balancing the information they received from government and the media.

If your corporation is interested in a programme of issue-oriented ads, you'll have to face the problem of tax deductibility, so I'll take a moment here to explain Mobil's position. By law, advertising is tax deductible if it 'presents views on economic, financial, social or other subjects of a general nature.' But if the ads constitute lobbying, or if they take a position on the passage or defeat of legislation, they are not tax deductible. To be safe, we take tax decisions for charity-related and public-service ads, but not for ads that deal with energy, the environment, or anything else even remotely connected with legislation. We submit all of our ads to counsel for their opinion on tax deductibility, and we've asked the lawyers to follow conservative standards.

At the same time, I've always been struck by what seems to be a blatant inequity. Why can a newspaper take a tax deduction for its editorials – including those that deal directly with legislation – while we at Mobil cannot? Why can a media corporation support a candidate while an industrial corporation cannot? To take an obvious example, most publications depend heavily on special third-class mailing privileges. And some of the larger publications are tied in to large conglomerates. Why do we assume that these parties are necessarily disinterested observers or that they are never involved in a conflict of interest? Eventually, when I retire and find myself in need of a project, I'd like to devote some time to looking into this question.

In recent years, corporate issue advertising has become increasingly popular. One reason for this development, I think, is that the media have been unable to cover complex issues – especially business issues – fully and accurately. As a result, both print and electronic journalism are full of distortions and simplifications that cry out to be corrected by advocacy advertising.

'Most advocacy campaigns,' writes David Ogilvy in *Ogilvy on Advertising*, 'are too little and too late. They are addressed to the wrong audience, lack a defined purpose, don't go on long enough, are weak in craftsmanship, and advocate a hopeless cause. So they fail.' Ogilvy's conclusion? Advocacy advertising is not a job for beginners.

Ogilvy is right to be cautious, but he overstates his case. For corporations interested in advocacy advertising, I would give the following advice: Stake out your objectives clearly. Be sure to define the issues you want to address. Make sure that your top management knows what is involved. They'll have to do more than approve the ads; they'll also have to take the heat. And if there's no heat, it's a sign that your ads aren't very effective.

To the extent that it's possible, try to run the entire programme yourself. If you have your ads prepared by an outside agency, they may be so slick as to turn off the people you want to reach. Instead, hire the best talent you can find, and put your energy into substance, style and timeliness. Finally, be patient: the results will not come overnight.

If you embark on an op-ed programme, it's important to develop a style that reflects your company's personality and to stick to it. Whatever style you use, be sure to talk to readers in terms they can personally identify with. Be consistent in what you say and how you say it. Check all your facts carefully. And above all, maintain your visibility. If you speak up only in times of crisis, your credibility is sure to suffer.

But enough theory. At this point, I'd like to present a few of my favourite 'advertorials' – together with a brief commentary on each one – from among the hundreds that Mobil has published over the past decade and a half.

When our op-ed programme began, we decided that we would occasionally take a broader view, and that we would discuss such topics as the nature of our economic system. What makes it viable? Why does it work? What could lead it to stop working?

The ad opposite represents a group of a dozen or so philosophical messages about capitalism that we've been running over the years. Initially, these ads were designed for two purposes. First, we wanted to help combat the massive amount of ignorance about our economic system. A great many Americans – including some who are otherwise well educated – simply do not understand how the free-market economy works, or why it has been so successful in our society.

Second, during the 1970s, we felt a pressing need to defend the free-market system at a time when its basic tenets were being called into question – especially among academics and intellectuals. In this ad and in others, we tried to speak directly to the concerns of the antibusiness reader.

Most of our ads are like conventional editorials in that we run them only once. But a few, like this one, are not time-bound, and every year or two we run them again.

Capitalism: moving target

The list of things wrong with business in this country is almost endless. Nearly as long, in fact, as the list of what's right with it.

Perhaps the most frustrating thing about business, for those who keep trying to shoot it down, is this: Corporations are so tenacious that they will even do good in order to survive. This tenacity goes beyond the old maxim that man, in his greed for profit, often unavoidably serves the public interest. In times of crisis, business will even do good *consciously* and *deliberately*.

Nothing could be better calculated to confound business's critics than this underhanded tactic. The Marxist dialectic has it that capitalism must inevitably founder in its own inherent contradictions; that it contains the seeds of its own destruction. But business also contains the seeds of its own adaptation and survival.

Businessmen are pragmatists, and with their daily feedback from the marketplace, they readily abandon dogma whenever their survival instinct tells them to. It has become less and less a question of what they *want* to do or might *like* to do, but of what their common sense and survival instinct tell them they *have* to do.

Remember the Edsel? That was one of the fastest plebiscites in history. But it wasn't the American public that took the loss; it was the shareholders of Ford Motor Company. (Then, you'll recall, Ford changed course and bounced back with the Mustang, which quickly showed its tailpipe to the competition by breaking all sales records for a new make of car.)

Because it is keyed so closely to the marketplace and so responsive to it, private business is necessarily the most effective instrument of change. Some would call it revolutionary. Many of those who attack business fail to comprehend its constructive contributions to responsive change. And this sort of change is one of the basic reasons business manages to survive.

Not *all* businesses survive, of course. The record is replete with companies that expired because they didn't adapt rapidly enough to a new milieu.

While businessmen as a whole are not exactly social reformers, they do respond to criticism and to sustained social pressures. The alert businessman regards such pressures as a useful early warning system. The danger is that criticism can become a mindless reflex action that persists long after the basis for it has been dissipated.

Partly because of its ability to adapt—which is simply another word for responsive change—private business remains the most productive element in our society and on balance the best allocator of resources. If you decide to draw a bead on it, remember you're aiming at a moving target. Because, as we've said here before, business is bound to change.

Mobil

Over the years, we have been deeply frustrated by the inability of the public or the press to distinguish between profits and profitability. It's true that in terms of actual dollars, the oil companies have usually made large profits. But everyone in business knows that the absolute size of a profit tells you nothing until you also know the size of the company reporting it.

Unfortunately, this basic information is not necessarily understood among the general public. Most people are surprised to learn that compared to the profitability of other industries, our rate of return has always been rather modest. Even in the so-called windfall years, our profit margins never got much above average.

Because profits are such an emotional issue, we have returned to this theme again and again. We've also stressed that to search for, refine, transport, and deliver new oil requires an enormous sum of money. And the only possible source for that money is our earnings.

While there's only room to reproduce one ad on this theme, some of our headlines have included:

We're one of the 10 biggest industrial corporations in the world.
You think that's big enough?
We're not so sure.

We're earning a lot.
We're spending more.
Sound familiar?

Are oil profits big?
Right.
Big enough?
Wrong.

If we tell you oil companies don't make enough profit, you'll have a fit. Oil companies don't make enough profit. Sorry.

The international oil industry has to find a new Kuwait every year, almost.

Between 1970 and 1971, oil consumption in the Free World increased by 2.2 million barrels a day. That approximates the petroleum output from Kuwait—one of the world's largest producers.

Oil consumption today is more than double what it was 10 years ago. And the world will use more oil in the Seventies than it used in all previous history.

To achieve the equivalent of a new Kuwait every year from here on, oil companies must invest money on a scale that boggles the mind. Mobil alone will make capital and exploration outlays of more than $1 billion this year.

For the past several years, oil companies have been unable to generate enough capital from their operations. They have been forced to borrow more and more of their capital needs; and the interest on loans, as well as the loan payments, adds significantly to the cost of doing business and eventually to product costs.

Of all sources of capital, net income—profit—is most important. To help provide the capital needed for investment, profit must grow as demand rises.

But for years, profits have grown much more slowly than demand. Between 1969 and 1971, while demand rose by 20 percent, aggregate net earnings of 30 of the world's largest oil companies increased by just over nine percent. In the same two-year period, worldwide tax payments of these companies went up by more than 50 percent.

One of the main reasons for inadequate earnings is that prices for U.S. petroleum products are too low. Too low for the consumer's own long-term interest. In June, 1972, the wholesale price of regular-grade gasoline in this country was only about five percent higher than in 1967, the base year used by the government for such surveys. Since 1967, the U.S. cost of living has risen more than 24 percent.

If oil companies are to have enough money in the years ahead to make the investments they must make to meet people's growing needs, their earnings will have to rise faster. There is just no other true solution.

If you understand this basic economic reality, maybe the next time somebody suggests that oil companies are not making enough profit, you won't have a fit.

Mobil®

During the two oil crises of the 1970s, the public was desperate for a scapegoat. And who would play that role better than the large oil companies? In the minds of those who chose to believe in a conspiracy, Mobil, Exxon, Shell, and all the rest had merged into one gigantic corporation of mythic proportions.

But while there are some huge companies in the oil business, the smaller companies and the independents have been steadily growing. And the majors have been losing ground.

At one point in the late 1970s, a number of proposals being considered in Congress called for government intervention to break up the major oil companies. Our purpose in this ad was to point out that the field was already a lot more crowded than most people realized. To survive as a national asset, we had to show that our industry was so competitive and diverse that no monopoly could exist.

43,141 companies have a monopoly on the U.S. oil business.

There are more, actually. We just got tired of counting.

We included companies that produce oil and refine and market their own products, and companies that perform only one or two of those functions.

We included independent wholesalers and fuel oil and liquefied petroleum gas distributors.

We omitted some 220,000 service stations, the vast majority of which are operated by independent businessmen.

But when some Americans think of the oil business, they count only six or seven companies. Cynics count those six or seven as one. And if you don't count past seven, or past one, it's easy to conclude that the oil business is a monopoly.

Funny monopoly. The biggest U.S. marketer of gasoline sells just over eight percent of the gasoline sold in this country. The average motorist can choose from 28 brands competing in his state. The interstate traveler could conceivably choose from among 180 brands of gasoline.

Some 15 of the larger oil companies are usually considered "majors." Each of them faces aggressive competition not only from the other companies in its league, but also from smaller "independents." In this latter competition, the majors have steadily lost ground. The independents' aggregate market position in gasoline, the petroleum product that moves in the largest volumes in this country, is up from 18.5 percent in 1966 to about 29 percent today.

The competition doesn't end—or even begin—with gasoline. Over 7,000 companies are in business to find and produce oil and natural gas, and the largest of them accounts for less than 10 percent of U.S. production.

The cost of a large, modern refinery, which can easily exceed $250 million, does not encourage thousands to enter that end of the business, but neither does any one firm dominate it. There are 239 refineries in this country, operated by 127 companies. The largest accounts for less than nine percent of total U.S. refining capacity. No other major manufacturing industry is so little "dominated" by any one company. Or any seven.

The oil business does include some of the world's largest industrial companies, Mobil among them. This industry breeds big companies because it takes an enormous complex of men and machines to meet the worldwide demand for energy. U.S. oil demand has more than doubled over the past 20 years, and it will almost double again by 1985. The world will require more oil just in the Seventies than in the past 100 years.

Competition clearly is good for the consumer. It has kept oil products—especially gasoline—among the best bargains in the marketplace. We think competition is good for the companies in the oil industry, too. It keeps us alert and responsive.

We face some of the toughest competitors in the world. We are determined not to let them monopolize the business.

Mobil®

This is one of my all-time favourites. The content was strong and the style was brilliant. But more than that – we took on a world-class media performer.

Early in 1974, Tom Wicker wrote an angry column in the *Times* that attacked the oil industry in general, and our advocacy ads in particular. Reading the column, I could see that while Tom Wicker didn't really like what we were doing, he hadn't put together much of an argument to make his point.

I immediately called my staff together and announced that we had to answer Wicker's column. The challenge here was not what to say, but to find the right format in which to say it. Charlie Pollak, one of the most creative writers we ever had, went out and wrote this one straight from the gut. Charlie insisted that it be typeset to look like it was done on a typewriter. He was right, of course, for here the medium is the message.

We've gone back to this format a number of times since, because it's an ideal way to express indignation, confusion, or anger. I'd like to think that the reader can visualize a fellow sitting at the typewriter, banging away in righteous indignation.

Musings of an oil person...

Wonder if oil company advertising isn't risking indecent overexposure these days. There's so much oil on the tube and in print. Gulf, Shell and Texaco all ran full-pagers on the same day last week in the Times. Mobil's on the Op-Ed page every Thursday. Why do we all do it? Some critics think the ads show the companies are conspiring to brainwash the public. Others think the advertising deluge proves we can't do anything right, not even conspire. But an oil company has to find some way of speaking its mind and letting the public know what's going on, especially now when oil companies are accused of being secretive. Have to take risk of moving Tom Wicker to nausea over the "...pious, self-serving, devious, mealy-mouthed, self-exculpating, holier-than-thou, positively sickening oil company advertisements in which these international behemoths depict themselves as poverty-stricken paragons of virtue embattled against a greedy and ignorant world." Tom turns a nice phrase, but doesn't he know we're frustrated in trying to get information to the public? Try to buy time on TV to say something substantive and the networks clobber you with the fairness doctrine. Same with radio. Several congressmen want the FTC to require a company to substantiate its idea advertising, just as if an idea were like a new toothpaste. Why don't they exhume Madison and make him substantiate the Bill of Rights? Sure, we can stick to print media to tell our story. But newspapers and magazines frequently don't understand the complexities of our industry. Only a few have oil specialists. And how many deadly news releases can we send them before they scream for mercy? Much better to use TV to try to reach the millions whose opinions about oil are swayed by what Cronkite, Chancellor and Reasoner say every evening. Briefly! In 30 seconds they can suggest enough wrongdoing that a year of full-page explanations by us won't set straight. Hate to be on the defensive all the time. Arm our top management people with facts and get them on TV panels and talk shows. They still look drab next to a politician making some wild allegation against us because he's running for something. Does he have to run on our backs? Sure he does--as long as there are gas lines. What do we tell the guy who's boiling mad at us--in our station or some other company's--after waiting two hours for the privilege of paying $1.10 for two gallons of gas? Are we going to tell him he's been wasting energy for years? No way. Tell him to lay off those jackrabbit starts? He'll find that out for himself. That Detroit's naughty for building big cars, that we shouldn't have built all those superhighways, that we're sorry we gave away all that glassware? Forget it. Should we remind him we've been warning for years that the energy crisis was coming? He'll mow down the pumps and who would blame him. No, have to focus on the positive things we can do. Tell him we're recycling the money he pays at the pump right back into oil-finding offshore, Alaska, anywhere. Into more refinery capacity. Into oil shale, synthetic fuels from coal, tar sands, far-out processes in the lab. Dammit, we're a can-do company in a can-do country. Give us a few years and we'll make gas lines just a quaint recollection of the mid-70s. In the meantime, try to reason with Washington against counter-productive laws and regulations. Fight the two-times-two-equals-five logicians who think the same outfit that brings you the U.S. Mail can find oil three miles under the ocean bottom. Give people the facts. Give them genuine information. Speak out. Persuade them to listen. Never bore them. If at first we don't succeed, bust a gut trying again. No other way. Or we all end up working for the government.

Mobil®

This delightful ad had its genesis during a discussion I had with Larry Woods, the former head of our corporate planning department. Larry was preparing his taxes one day, and he called me to announce that the government had just figured out a way to create money. We had a good laugh over it, but we were also angry at the government's apparently willingness to mislead people about our system of taxes and expenditures.

If that extra dollar wasn't coming out of our taxes, where was it coming from? Had this kind of sloppy thinking appeared in a private-sector document, the Federal Trade Commission would have gone after the perpetrator for violating truth-in-packaging laws.

After our phone call, I realized that this discussion could be the basis of an effective ad. The format we chose seemed to be a light and charming way to make two serious points: first, that every dollar spent has to come from somewhere, and second, that the federal financing of elections may not be such a great idea. This ad received a lot of attention and was a particular favourite of columnists and commentators..

The cloning of a dollar

You probably did a double take—just like the rest of us—when you read this line on your Form 1040.

Presidential Election Campaign	Do you want $1 to go to this fund?	Yes	No	**Note:** *Checking "Yes" will not increase your tax or reduce your refund*
	If joint return, does your spouse want $1 to go to this fund?	Yes	No	

The clear implication is that those wonderful folks in Washington have now passed into a fourth dimension—let us call it The Fiscal Zone—in which they can create money out of nothing. And not only that: they are now inviting all the rest of us, via Form 1040, to join them in that magical, mystical place.

Let's see, now.

You will give them a dollar, but it will not increase your tax. Where will it come from, this dollar for the Presidential Election Campaign? Obviously not from you. And obviously not from the money that actually belongs to you but that has been collected and held by the government—because that money is your refund, and your giving of this dollar will not reduce your refund. It says so right there on the 1040.

Wow!

We are manifestly trembling here, along with the government, on the verge of one of those vast invisible secrets like The Law of Diminishing Returns. We suppose it may become known as The Law of Procreating Returns, because the language on this tax form demonstrates that Washington can now get money—can in some peculiar fashion actually grow money—without increasing your taxes.

But...whence comes this free dollar? Surely our leaders will not claim they divert it from some less worthy end to the Presidential Election Campaign—because any such diverted dollar certainly is a dollar of taxes. If they can limp along without the less worthy end, they could limp along without your dollar. Therefore, it can't be a dollar that our friends on the Potomac are merely moving from Column A to Column B.

And surely it can't be a dollar they're getting from your neighbor's tax, rather than yours. If you check the campaign block, and he doesn't, does that mean your taxes don't go up but his refund is less than it would have been? (Maybe you'd better not say anything to your neighbors about this.) But that dollar is a tax dollar, too, whether it comes from your house or the one next door. Taxes are taxes: we all pay them, and if the total is reduced by a diverted dollar, then one of us, or all of us, is chipping in to cover the reduction.

So it's not taken from your neighbor. And it's not taken from another government program. And it's not taken from you.

We can't conceive that the tooth fairy brought it—and must conclude Washington has discovered that dollars breed. You put them in a drawer, in the dark, and soon there are two where only one was before. This is no doubt the secret behind the dollar we get to allocate on the 1040. Fascinating: not a word about it in the media and yet truly a miracle—the cloning of a dollar.

What next?

Mobil®

One day Rawleigh Warner asked me out of the blue, 'Do you think you could do some fables?'

'I don't know,' I replied. 'It sounds like an interesting idea, so we'll give it a try.' Over time, we turned out seven or eight little stories. Our fables attracted a lot of attention – not all of it favourable. While some people thought they were brilliant, our opponents insisted they were manipulative.

In my view, the real problem for our opponents is that we dared to present a moral to our story – a concept they thought they owned. Moreover, the probusiness forces did not normally use such 'creative' techniques to get their point across, which was another reason why some people hated the fables. It was after this fable appeared that I formulated Schmertz's Seventh Law: The opposition will always defend your right to free speech so long as you have no hope of convincing anyone.

When this ad appeared, we were involved in a debate over price controls on energy. In our view, price controls would have provided no economic incentive to develop new sources of energy. But had we framed our argument in those terms, who would have listened? With the fables, we were able to make the problem understandable and even interesting to people who had no inherent interest in business. It was a communications breakthrough, as we were no longer preaching to the choir.

A Fable For Now:

How the squirrel found himself up a tree.

There once was a squirrel who collected nuts and stored them. In this way, he was able to see himself safely through the long, hard, cold winters.

Other squirrels soon noticed how good he was at finding nuts, collecting them, and bringing them home. So they asked if he would do the same for them. They, in turn, agreed to pay him for his services.

Soon, he was finding and delivering nuts to squirrels near and far. As might be expected, nuts became harder and harder for the squirrel to find. Because the search became more difficult, it cost him more. (He had by now devised an ingenious transportation system to move nuts from one squirrel community to another.) So he raised the price he charged the other squirrels.

This, of course, caused some concern, particularly among those squirrels who weren't familiar with the nut gatherer's problems. Because they never had to look for nuts, they thought nuts must be awfully easy to find, harvest, and deliver. And so they appealed to the Supreme Squirrel.

He, in his wisdom, determined that a Furry Persons' Committee should determine what price the squirrel should charge for his nuts. The Committee set a low price, and all the other squirrels thought that decision was, in their words, "a real gasser."

"Now we won't have to shell out so much," they said.

On the other hand, the nut-gathering squirrel wasn't too crazy about the price that was set.

"Why should I knock myself out?" he said. "This is tough work, and if I can't squirrel away a little something for myself, I'd be crazy to look for nuts in hard-to-find places."

And so, his incentive gone, he stopped searching in those hard-to-find places. Pretty soon, he began to run out of nuts. Naturally, he started cutting back on deliveries to far-away squirrels. And, naturally, his customers were upset. They couldn't understand why there were not enough nuts to go around.

So, the first squirrel patiently explained: "You wanted nuts on your terms, and as long as I could supply them to you on that basis, I did. Because nuts were so cheap you used more and more. Now, they're just too expensive to find. Unless you get the Furry Persons' Committee to stop telling me what price I can charge, you're going to have to get along with fewer nuts."

Moral: When the Supreme Squirrel interferes with the pricing of nuts, it's enough to drive you up a tree. Which reminds us: The U.S. is still suffering from the Supreme Court's 1954 decision to let the Federal Power Commission regulate the price of natural gas shipped across state lines. In the government's eagerness to keep prices low, it hurt the industry's incentive to find more gas. Only decontrol of new natural gas can restore that incentive. And that's no fable.

Mobil

During the national debate over divestiture, we wanted to point out that opposition to the breakup of the major oil companies was not limited to those of us with an obvious interest in preserving the status quo. We knew that we had to argue the case in terms of the public's interest, rather than the vested interest of the major oil companies.

In the spring of 1978, a number of newspapers, radio outlets, and television stations had gone on record saying that divestiture was a bad idea. We decided to reprint selections from their statements in an ad whose overall effect would suggest a unity of opinion from widely different sources.

In retrospect, our decision to reproduce the logos of the publications and stations who supported our position probably doubled the effectiveness of this ad.

Voices of reason

A growing number of voices are being raised against proposals in the Congress to break up the large oil companies into smaller, less efficient units.

People without axes to grind. People outside the oil industry. Radio and television commentators and editorials. Newspaper editorials.

Of the editorials we've come across so far, more than 60 oppose divestiture, and only one urged passage of the legislation.

Here are samples:

THE ARIZONA REPUBLIC "Breaking up the oil companies would be a national disaster."

KNBC Los Angeles: "The over-riding fact is that bigness in oil companies isn't necessarily bad, when it takes billions of dollars in risk capital to go get the oil we all seem to want to keep using. If the politicians who're trying to climb into higher office over the bodies of America's oil companies really want to cut your fuel prices, we think they should stop monkeying around with more regulations and break-up threats, and let the forces of competition decide how big and how integrated an oil company should be." **The Los Angeles Times** also came out against divestiture.

THE KANSAS CITY STAR "The people pushing divestiture are not doing anything to ease the energy shortage or bring down prices; they are just playing to the political galleries by trying to sock it to Big, Bad Oil."

The Hartford Times "The effort by some liberal congressmen to force divestiture is so laughable that the initial inclination is to ignore the rantings as petty demagoguery. Unfortunately, history has proven that petty demagoguery, when ignored, all too often can succeed in achieving incredibly destructive ends."

WLOS-TV-FM of Greenville, S.C.: "The philosophy behind these proposals is that 'big is bad,' which ignores the fact that big is almost always more efficient and productive ... More often than not, bigness benefits the consumer." In neighboring North Carolina, Charlotte's WBT and WBTV added: "Sure, there are about 20 oil companies that are mighty big. But it's because they're big that they've been able to afford the exploration, the drilling and the sophisticated distribution system that provided America for so long with cheap, dependable fuel—and that, even now, has kept us from being utterly swamped by the 500% increase in OPEC oil prices."

THE SPOKESMAN-REVIEW of Spokane: "A Federal Energy Administration study indicates that requiring oil companies to split up would result in less production and higher prices to consumers. If this is true, it would be a clearcut case of cutting off one's nose to spite one's face."

THE INDIANAPOLIS STAR "The industry as presently structured has served the nation very well. It could continue to do so if government would let it alone."

TULSA DAILY WORLD "At a time when the country faces a growing and dangerous shortage of domestic fuel supplies, it would seem incredible that Congress would attempt to punish people who are investing their money and talent in the search for new sources."

DESERET NEWS of Salt Lake City: "... instead of trying to break up oil companies, the government should get on with the job of formulating a rational and comprehensive national energy policy."

San Francisco Chronicle "Once big oil is broken up, who's next? It is logical to expect that the line will form on the left, of course, to bust up the automobile industry, steel, aluminum, the computer industry, and anything else big and inviting."

If you'd like a full file of editorials on this issue, write to:
Mobil Oil Corporation, Box E, 150 E. 42nd Street, New York, NY 10017.

Mobil

I've always felt that to use our op-ed space only to push our own agenda and debate our critics would constitute the abuse of a special privilege. For that reason, and in order to reveal other facets of our personality, we have used our space to support a variety of causes, including the United Negro College Fund, the New York Urban Coalition, the Interracial Council for Business Opportunity, Jobs for Veterans, the Better Business Bureau, and many other groups. We have also taken out ads to support quality television programmes for children, such as *Sesame Street* and *The Electric Company*. And in a number of cities, we have taken ads to call attention to local art groups.

The CPR programme was something that we at Mobil had already become involved with, and our purpose here was to urge people in other organizations to learn this lifesaving skill.

Training to live

Cardiopulmonary resuscitation is a mouthful, which is why CPR is its common name. What it means, in hundreds of cases, is life instead of death.

CPR is the most effective means yet devised through which a trained layman—like you—can sustain the life of a heart attack victim, or a person who has been electrocuted, or has stopped breathing. What CPR does is keep the victim alive until expert help can arrive on the scene.

The key, of course, is the presence of the trained layman—and training is the key to CPR's effectiveness. That's why in companies across the nation, Mobil included, thousands of employees have completed a basic course in CPR.

The course teaches a general familiarity with anatomy and physiology. Students learn to recognize the symptoms of a heart attack and, by working on mannequins, how to sustain vital functions until the experts reach the scene. What they learn is also useful in cases of choking, shock, bleeding, burns, poisoning, and drug overdoses.

Above all else, practitioners of CPR are able to buy time. They're people who keep other people alive when seconds count. Their slogan: "A minute saved is a life saved."

All across the country, groups like the American Heart Association, the American Red Cross, and local police departments, fire departments, and ambulance corps are offering CPR training. Want a good town to need help in? In Seattle, Washington, some 60 percent of the general population has had CPR training.

Mobil's headquarters program was given under the direction of our Medical Department, and conducted by the Empire State Ambulance Service, of New York City. Among our participants were the chairman of the board, the president, several directors, and their wives—400 employees and their family members. We easily met our objective of having trained personnel on every floor of our headquarters building, and we've since trained people at our other Mobil facilities.

Frankly, wouldn't you feel easier if your neighbor had CPR training? Wouldn't he or she enjoy the security of knowing you're trained?

What's stopping you? Get involved in CPR. The time you spend may be the most important investment you've ever made.

Mobil

Late in 1971, the New York Public Library announced that its Science and Technology Division was in imminent danger of closing down owing to a shortage of funds. This particular section of the library has always been of enormous importance to the business community, and we felt strongly that it deserved corporate support. In addition to making our own contribution, we used this ad to encourage other corporations to add their support. The response was terrific, and the Science and Technology Division was able to remain open. I only wish all our ads fell upon such willing ears!

Help wanted. Urgent.

This isn't an employment ad.

It is an urgent call for help.

The New York Public Library needs $86,000 in a hurry.

If the library cannot raise that amount by the end of this week, it will be forced to close its Science and Technology Division to students, researchers, and the general public.

This priceless asset that has made such a great contribution to intellectual and commercial life must not be lost for want of $86,000.

We urge the city, the state, banks, foundations, other corporations, and you to join with us and others who are aiding the library.

Send your tax-deductible contribution to Richard W. Couper, President, New York Public Library, Fifth Avenue at 42nd Street, New York City 10018.

Checks should be made out to: NYPL-Science & Technology.

Do it today.

Please.

The need is urgent.

Mobil®

This ad turned out to be one of the most controversial messages we've ever run. Owing to the nature of the oil business, our information from the Middle East tends to be fairly reliable. In 1973, we had the strong impression that tensions between Israel and the Arab world were close to the boiling point. But we were concerned that our own government did not perceive this risk as being real. When we approached the State Department with our concerns, they told us not to be alarmists.

We thought it important to point out that America, too, had a stake in Middle East peace, if for no other reason than the prospect of a major disruption in our oil supplies in the event of war – a possibility that in our view was growing more likely every week. The ad did not mention Israel because we didn't want to focus here on the rights and wrongs of the Arab-Israeli conflict. The issue at hand was simply the future of America's oil supply, which boiled down to the need for recognizing the strategic importance of Saudi Arabia. Our critics accused us of running this ad at the behest of the Saudis, but there was no truth to this charge.

Three and a half months after this ad appeared, war erupted in the Middle East. It was followed by the Arab oil embargo.

The U.S. stake in Middle East peace: I

Oil and natural gas supply over three-quarters of the energy used in the United States.

Our society literally cannot live without adequate oil supplies. We could not even grow our own food without oil to power farm machines, much less continue as an industrial society.

U.S. oil consumption is rising rapidly and will continue to, even though we must become much more efficient in our use of energy. Yet domestic production of crude oil is actually declining now. We already have to depend on other countries for over a third of the oil we use. In another seven years, or less, we will be relying on foreign sources for more than half our oil.

This is the prospect even if a pipeline is built to bring oil from Alaska's North Slope to market in this country, and even if large additional oil reserves are found and produced off the U.S. East and West Coasts.

Canada, Venezuela, and Nigeria, among others, are substantial exporters of oil to the U.S., and increasing volumes of their oil will probably come here. The North Sea is a promising area, but this oil will be consumed in Northwest Europe. Additional new oil provinces in various parts of the world will probably be brought into production over the coming years.

However, based on everything we now know, the Middle East is the only region in the world with large enough reserves of oil to meet the inevitable increase in U.S. consumption. Like it or not, the United States is dependent on the Middle East even just to maintain our present living standards in the years immediately ahead.

Of all the countries in the Middle East, the U.S. must look primarily to Saudi Arabia and Iran for oil. Each of these countries has its own unique needs and problems and opportunities; later in this series, we will have more to say about this.

Of these two countries, Saudi Arabia has the most oil—more, in fact, than any other nation in the world. Its reserves can support an increase from the present production level of about 8 million barrels a day to 20 million barrels daily. Iran's reserves can support an increase in production from about 6 million barrels a day now to around 9 million barrels daily. Mobil has substantial interests in the oil reserves of both countries—and substantial supply obligations to millions of customers around the world.

We in the United States must learn to live with the peoples of these two countries and to understand that they look to us for policies that recognize their legitimate interests and aspirations. If we want to continue to enjoy our present life style, or anything approaching it, then—no matter how much more efficient we may become in the use of energy—we will have to understand the changed and still-changing conditions in the Middle East and in the rest of the world.

If our country's relations with the Arab world (Iran is not an Arab state) continue to deteriorate, Saudi Arabia may conclude it is not in its interest to look favorably on U.S. requests for increased petroleum supplies. The government of that country has the power to decide how much oil is to be produced within its borders. And to what countries that oil can be shipped.

In the last analysis, political considerations may become the critical element in Saudi Arabia's decisions, because we will need the oil more than Saudi Arabia will need the money. That country could reduce oil exports 3 million barrels a day below *present* levels and, with its small population, still finance its domestic development programs with a comfortable margin for reserves. Its present reserves of foreign exchange—dollars, pounds sterling, and gold—exceed $3 billion and will reach about $5 billion by the end of this year.

Thus Saudi Arabia has no urgent financial incentive to increase oil production to 20 million barrels a day, or even to increase it at all.

It is therefore time for the American people to begin adapting to a new energy age, to a vastly changed world situation, to the realities with which we will have to learn to live. Nothing less than clear thinking, a sense of urgency, and a grasp of what is at risk can lay the base for achieving a durable peace in the Middle East.

So we say: It is time now for the world to insist on a settlement in the Middle East, backed by ironclad and credible guarantees from the United States and the Soviet Union, among others. A settlement that will bring justice and security to all the peoples and all the states of that region. Nobody can afford another war in the Middle East. Nobody. *Nobody.*

None of us can any longer go on just hoping the situation in that part of the world will somehow resolve itself peacefully. Because the alternatives to a just, peaceful, and lasting resolution have become intolerable.

Mobil®

In the spring of 1980, the Public Broadcasting Service decided to show a British docudrama called *Death of a Princess*. The show told the story of a princess in an unnamed country – it was clearly Saudi Arabia – who had an illicit love affair and was subsequently beheaded by the authorities.

I was familiar with the show, which had previously been aired in England. In the guise of a documentary, *Death of a Princess* had perpetuated a libel about the people and religion of Saudi Arabia. Moreover, the showing of the film on British television had led to strong diplomatic protests from the Saudis and adversely affected British commercial interests in that country.

We ran this ad only after the most serious and careful consideration, and only after we concluded that some statement had to be made about the nature of the show. We were fully aware that by running the ad we would be giving *Death of a Princess* a great deal of publicity, which would probably serve to increase its audience.

But we also felt that it was important to be clear about the consequences of the show. Among other problems, the fact that *Death of a Princess* was being aired on public television might lead other nations to believe that it enjoyed the support of our government. In fact, the State Department deplored the programme. But we were doubtful as to whether America's unique separation of powers would necessarily be appreciated abroad.

Naturally, our opponents claimed that we were trying to intimidate the Public Broadcasting Service and that we had tried to prevent the show from airing. At no point did we make any attempt to stop the show, either through the ad or through other channels. Our goal wasn't to censor *Death of a Princess*, but rather to let the viewing public know that this particular story was also libellous and offensive to one of our strategic allies.

A new fairy tale

On May 12, a number of Public Broadcasting Service stations are scheduled to show a television film which purports to depict certain events and practices in Saudi Arabia. When this film was aired several weeks ago in Britain, it caused Saudi Arabia to express its objections to the British Government. In Saudi Arabia's view, the film misrepresented its social, religious, and judicial systems and, in effect, was insulting to an entire people and the heritage of Islam.

As a consequence, the following transpired:

- According to *The New York Times*, the British Foreign Secretary sent a letter to Prince Saud Al-Faisal, the Saudi Foreign Minister, expressing his "profound regret."
- *The Times* also reported that the British Foreign Office issued the following statement:

"It is most unfortunate that Anglo-Saudi relations should have been damaged by a film for which the British Government was in no way responsible and which it could not prevent from being shown on British television or elsewhere. We hope it will be possible to restore relations on their normal level as soon as possible."

In our opinion, the proposed showing of this film on public television in the United States raises some very serious issues:

1. If we are going to have a free press, what responsibilities and obligations to the well-being of the nation does that freedom impose upon television stations and other media?

2. What are the implications of the fact that congressional appropriations to public television supported, at least indirectly, the production of the film and, if shown, the facilities for dissemination?

3. Does the public regard fictionalized "docu-drama" accounts loosely based on some historical event as accurate portrayals of those events, even though fiction is mixed with so-called fact? Many serious commentators have raised questions about the "docu-drama" format.

We believe that if a free society is to survive, we must openly and candidly discuss these issues so that an informed public may make rational judgments.

1. Obligations of a Free Press

We all know that in the U.S., our Constitution guarantees a free and unfettered press. However, implicit in that guarantee is the obligation on the part of the press to be responsible. Clearly, the people of the U.S. have the right to expect that the media will not abuse its privilege. The public will have to decide whether a "free press" is acting responsibly if it presents a fictionalized story of "events" and thereby demeans another nation's religion and possibly jeopardizes U.S. relations with that nation.

2. The Role of Government Support

Here we have a curious contradiction. Congressional appropriations have indirectly made possible the television structure which helped produce and will disseminate the show. We are not suggesting that congressional grants to public television should contain substantive restrictions nor are we suggesting our government in any way is responsible for the film. We know, however, that other nations may not understand how one branch of the government may deplore or regret a film offensive to a friendly country while another unwittingly supports it financially.

3. The "Reality" of Docu-drama

It should be understood that this film is not a news documentary. Rather, it is a drama using actors whose roles and dialogue have been scripted by a writer and, both in terms of visual portrayal and dialogue, must be classified as fiction. Yet, the claim will be that it is a factual presentation of a series of events. In this case, we are not dealing with the rights of a free press to express its views. Rather, we are dealing with a controversial film which most of the viewing audience will take as fact and thereby reach incorrect conclusions. Many television reviewers have raised serious doubts about this type of television which so blurs the distinction between fact and fiction that the viewer doesn't know one from the other.

This issue was discussed in a letter to *The New Statesman* by Penelope Mortimer who worked with Antony Thomas, the show's producer: "I was involved with the project for almost a year, and present at most of the interviews. I accompanied Thomas on his ten-day trip to Saudi Arabia, and was with him in Beirut in September 1978. With the exception of Barry Milner, who had already sold his story to the *Daily Express*, Rosemary Buschow, and the Palestinian family in Beirut, every interview and every character in the film is fabricated. The 'revelation' of the domestic lives of the Saudi princesses—man-hunting in the desert, rendezvous in boutiques—was taken entirely on the evidence of an expatriate divorcée, as was the story of the princess first seeing her lover on Saudi television. No real effort was made to check up on such information. Rumour and opinion somehow came to be presented as fact . . . the audience, foolishly believing it to be authentic, is conned."

That is why we say the show is a new fairy tale.

4. Conclusion

We hope that the management of the Public Broadcasting Service will review its decision to run this film, and exercise responsible judgment in the light of what is in the best interest of the United States.

Mobil®

This ad is one of my favourites, and I can't understand why we didn't think of running it years earlier. By 1981, our programme of advocacy ads had become a popular topic of discussion in the press, the business world, and even in the universities. There was a considerable amount of speculation as to why, exactly, we had embarked on the programme, and so to what we stood to gain from it. In view of this, I thought it would be a good idea to address the issue straight-on. In the process, of course, we revealed another level of our corporate personality.

Why do we buy this space?

For more than 12 years now, we've been addressing Americans with weekly messages in principal print media. We've argued, cajoled, thundered, pleaded, reasoned and poked fun. In return, we've been reviled, revered, held up as a model and put down as a sorry example.

Why does Mobil choose to expose itself to these weekly judgments in the court of public opinion? Why do we keep it up now that the energy crisis and the urgent need to address energy issues have eased, at least for the present?

Our answer is that business needs voices in the media, the same way labor unions, consumers, and other groups in our society do. Our nation functions best when economic and other concerns of the people are subjected to rigorous debate. When our messages add to the spectrum of facts and opinion available to the public, even if the decisions are contrary to our preferences, then the effort and cost are worthwhile.

Think back to some of the issues in which we have contributed to the debate.

- Excessive government regulation—it's now widely recognized that Washington meddling, however well intentioned, carries a price tag that the consumer pays.
- The folly of price controls—so clear now that prices of gasoline and other fuels are coming down, now that the marketplace has been relieved of most of its artificial restraints.
- The need for balance between maintaining jobs and production and maintaining a pristine environment—a non-issue, we argued, if there's common sense and compromise on both sides, a view that's now increasingly recognized in Washington.

Over the years, we've won some and lost some, and battled to a draw on other issues we've championed, such as building more nuclear power plants and improving public transportation. We've supported presidents we thought were right in their policies and questioned Democrats and Republicans alike when we thought their policies were counterproductive.

In the process we've had excitement, been congratulated and castigated, made mistakes, and won and lost some battles. But we've enjoyed it. While a large company may seem terribly impersonal to the average person, it's made up of people with feelings, people who care like everybody else. So even when we plug a quality TV program we sponsor on public television, we feel right about spending the company's money to build audience for the show, just as we feel good as citizens to throw the support of our messages to causes we believe in, like the Mobil Grand Prix, in which young athletes prepare for this year's Olympics. Or recognition for the positive role retired people continue to play in our society.

We still continue to speak on a wide array of topics, even though there's no immediate energy crisis to kick around anymore. Because we don't want to be like the mother-in-law who comes to visit only when she has problems and matters to complain about. We think a continuous presence in this space makes sense for us. And we hope, on your part, you find us informative occasionally, or entertaining, or at least infuriating. But never boring. After all, you did read this far, didn't you?

Mobil®

This ad is a good example of how we used 'Observations' to discuss some of our negative experiences with the press. The tone is more informal that our op-ed ads, and the whole texture of the ad is very different. And yet the content is similar to what we are saying each week in the *Times*.

Observations

Good news blues. *"All I know is just what I read in the papers,"* cracked humorist Will Rogers back in the 1920s. Today, some things that you don't read in newspapers, or see on network TV news, are what you ought to know–especially about **energy**, a field where reporters too often go **tilting at windmills.** Well, as a top journalist put it, *"bad news sells better."*

Silent knights. For much of the media, *"covering"* the oil industry means putting a wet blanket on good cheer. A recent example–the heavy silence that greeted government economist Richard Greene's report in the Labor Department's May *Monthly Labor Review.* Rising energy costs mean more additional sources of energy, he said...more gas and oil wells completed in six months last year than in all of 1973...more jobs created in the U.S. oil and natural gas industry–almost 50 percent more after rigid price controls began to soften. Quite a contrast to the crusading critics' charges that the oil industry squanders money on *"department stores and circuses."*

"And that's the opinion of the management of this station..."

Surprise! Sometimes good news is so astounding that the media may be too dazed to report it. Take the recent revelation from Harvard's Energy and Environmental Policy Center. Seems U.S. oil companies **undercharged customers by $5 billion** during the supply crisis following the Iranian revolution. *"We were surprised ourselves,"* said one of the report's authors. But *"the data is clear... major [oil company] prices fell behind the rest."* The reason for the big companies' lagging prices? Pressure from the media and threats from politicians going *"after the most visible and thus the largest"* targets. So who's ripping off whom?

A little learning.... If the media had properly covered either of these studies (and admitted that some past stories about oil industry "wrongdoings" were inaccurate), you and the rest of the public would have benefited. Some media-watchers have suggested that the fairy tales concocted by *"energy experts"* could be eliminated if reporters go to school to bone up on energy. Not a bad idea, especially now, when kids are hitting the books again. After all, as the poet Alexander Pope said: *"A little learning is a dangerous thing."*

It's a fact: Oil industry profits are big news in the media... but both publishing and broadcasting have been more profitable than oil over the past five years, based on return on stockholders' equity.

Mobil®

SEVEN

Surviving in Washington

ONE REASON WHY OPINION makers are so important in our national culture is that, eventually, their ideas and arguments trickle down to Washington. As a public, Washington is at least as important as the press, and often more so, as no other constituency is likely to have as great an affect on whatever institution, cause, or industry you represent. With Washington, as with the press, you have a choice: you can maintain a low profile and allow the government and its various agencies to damage our organization, or you can maintain a high profile and take an active confrontational role when such a posture is appropriate. To me, the choice is obvious.

Washington is a beautiful city, but it's a poor choice for our nation's capital. In most developed countries around the world, the centre of government is also the centre of the national economy, culture and population. Think of London, Paris, Rome, Tokyo, Moscow, Peking, Cairo. Washington, by contrast, is an artifical creation, and is actually little more than an overgrown small town.

Some years back, people used to say that Washington was a place of northern charm and southern efficiency. While there's still some truth to that notion, over the past two decades the city has grown far more lively and cosmopolitan. You no longer see Velveeta cheese in the gourmet section of the supermarket, for example, and the restaurants have improved tremendously. Congress is no longer dominated by sleepy long-term southern Democrats who have been around for twenty terms. And the press no longer drives over to Annapolis in the afternoon for a day of sailing, confident that nothing important will happen while they're away.

At the same time, Washington isn't exactly buzzing with speed and activity. Anyone who arrives in the capital from a highly disciplined business environment or from New York City will have to learn to slow down. That's because Washington is the only city in America whose primary business lacks a profit motive. As a result, there is no reward for efficiency. Have you ever stood in line at the post office to register a letter? There are times when all of Washington resembles a gigantic post office. In other words, don't expect to accomplish too much in one day.

Washington moves slowly for political reasons, too. The large bureaucracy is one part of the problem. So is the process of legislation: the city is filled with so many representatives of special-interest groups that their major effect is less to affect legislation than to slow it down. As a result of the various pressures on them, legislators have become increasingly cautious. Moreover, the vast number of issues before a legislator means that he can't know very much about any one of them. In short, the political and legislative agendas are so massive and complex that nobody can wade through them very fast.

Washington is a company town. The fact that the entire city is built around a single industry leads to a fair amount of provincialism and insulation. The permanent bureaucrats who run Washington and the journalists who report on it are never exposed to any industry other than government. As a result, they spend their working lives without any real interaction with the worlds of business, commerce, or labour. This is a city without grease or gristle. Anywhere else, you'd be meeting people who make things – whether it's cars or carpets or canoes. But in Washington, just about the only things that are manufactured are policy and gossip.

Although on the surface they're very different, Washington has a lot in common with Hollywood. Both cities revolve around a single industry that has little in common with the rest of the nation. Both are served by a trade paper: the *Washington Post* is to Washington what *Variety* is to Hollywood. Both cities run to gossip. And both cities foster an unusually high degree of that special paranoia that is generated by successful but insecure people who are always looking over their shoulder to see who's gaining on them. In Hollywood you're only as good as your last movie; in Washington you're only as good as your last election.

Washington is like Hollywood in another way, too, in that the line separating work and recreation is blurry at best. Often, it doesn't exist at all. Charitable and recreational events and entertaining are generally seen and used for political purposes, to the point that Washington may be the only city in America where social invitations are routinely sent to the office. (A well-placed and active couple may receive a hundred or more invitations a week.) Even the cultural life of Washington is little more than an appendage of the business of government. This becomes clear in the arts coverage of the *Washington Post*: what really counts is not the event itself, but the list of all the famous and powerful people who showed up.

WHY COME TO WASHINGTON?

In addition to your corporation's regular presence in Washington, there are various reasons for having one or more of your top people come to town. You may be trying to achieve or defeat the passage of a specific piece of legislation. You may be trying to build a long-term relationship with one or more legislators, or with their staffs. You may be trying to help reelect or defeat a member of Congress. You may be trying to support or oppose a politician with presidential ambitions. You may be interested in building an ongoing relationship with opinion-making journalists or columnists. You may want to achieve favourable publicity for a project, a product, a policy, or a cultural event. Or you may be interested in sending a message to a particular group of people – or even to a single member of Congress or the administration.

HOW TO GET ALONG IN WASHINGTON

The two best guides to life in Washington are Yogi Berra and Woody Allen. 'Always go to other people's funerals,' Berra once said. 'Otherwise, they won't come to yours.' In other words, Washington is a city of reciprocity: you scratch my back and I'll scratch yours. Among legislators, there is an old tradition of log-rolling, whereby members agree to support each other's pet projects. A similar arrangement is in effect among lobbyists. So always think in terms of potential alliances, especially with people whose interests may be different from yours.

When Woody Allen observed that 90 per cent of life's success consists of showing up, he must have been thinking of Washington. For this is a city of contacts, and its important to go places, to be seen, to be making new connections continually. Having the right social style is critical in Washington, where most entertaining is done at home, in the evening. In a town that makes no real distinction between work and leisure, the Washington political salon remains a unique and powerful institution. Anywhere else, such a gathering would be merely one more dinner party. But here, there is a great deal of power and prestige in the ability to attract and bring together a good mix of people. These are essentially political events, and as such they have nothing to do with friendship.

Similarly, there are a great many charities and cultural groups in Washington, and most of the important people in town are active in at least one of them. You may want to get directly involved in the group of your choice, not only because you value the cause or institution, but because you know full well that the meetings and social functions of these groups invariably provide opportunities for good contracts.

For these reasons, Washington is a very easy city for a newcomer to break into. It seems that almost everybody who counts in Washington comes from somewhere else, and sooner or later they all go back home. New faces are the norm here, as the cast of characters changes every two years, with each congressional election.

The only thing more important than who you know in Washington is *what* you know. In Washington, information is as important as money. In fact, information *is* money: it's the local currency. People in Washington acquire information, hoard it, spend it, and trade it just as the rest of us do with dollars. The name of the game in this town is to make the other guy feel as though he's missed the briefing.

Washington may be the only city in the world where sound travels faster than light. In other words, this is a hard place to keep a secret. Washington revolves around gossip, and it's almost impossible to stay clear of it. In part this is because the whole town is a fishbowl: every other person is a journalist, and they're all interested in the same stories. Is there any other city in America where two of the restaurants are named Whispers and Rumors?

Gossip can be fun, but it can also be dangerous. The major institutions in Washington and the people who staff them have an enormous capacity for being destructive. The reasons for this are more political than ideological, as many politicians spend a great deal of their time and energy trying to make their colleagues look bad. The same holds true for congressional staffs, who are always trying to sabotage their counterparts on the other side of the aisle. Even the permanent bureaucracy frequently engages in activities that are designed to undermine the workings of government. They're playing politics too, because every political appointment threatens another job. But for sheer destructiveness, you can't beat the Washington press corps, which thrives on destroying both reputations and careers.

Another rule to keep in mind in Washington is that people get attention only because of the institution they represent. Not surprisingly, this is often difficult for them to accept. After all, it's only natural to attribute some of your success and prestige to your own talent and personality. That's why the worst thing that can happen to any bright young person is to work in the White House before turning thirty. Such people often spend the rest of their lives trying to recapture that experience.

GETTING YOUR CASE HEARD ON CAPITOL HILL

The first thing to keep in mind about Congress is that a legislator's reelection campaign begins on his first day in office. This is especially true for members of the House, who must face a new election every two years. Job security is precarious on Capitol Hill; somebody is always gunning for your job.

As a result, the visitor who comes to Washington to lobby for or against legislation, or simply to talk to a legislator, must always put himself in the other fellow's situation. Try to empathize with the many conflicting pressures that the congressman or senator is facing. Unless he's genuinely uncommitted, don't even try to get him to change his position. Instead, help him find a position he can live with. To do this, you must help him find a resolution that avoids a head-on confrontation with his constituents, his staff, or his party colleagues. Remember: your goal is not to write a new symphony, but merely to strike a responsive chord.

The second thing you should understand about congressmen and senators is that they are strongly influenced by several different groups. First, there is the office staff, which is headed up by an administrative assistant who runs the office and directs the legislators's political and constituent activities. Most legislators also have an assistant who is responsible for press relations. Next comes the legislative assistant, who is responsible for keeping the member abreast of current legislative issues and debates, and who is usually the member's key substantive adviser. Another influence on the legislator is the committee on which he sits, and the staff members of that committee.

Finally, there is the home office. As House Speaker Thomas ('Tip') O'Neill likes to remind the younger members, 'All politics is local.' Every legislator maintains an office back home that is responsible for dealing with constituents and their problems. An active and successful member of Congress generally spends a lot of his time meeting with and listening to the people he represents. Legislators are usually telling the truth when they say to you, 'Personally, I agree with your position, but my constituents would never go along.'

Unless you actually live in Washington, you may not be aware that the congressional staff wields a great deal of behind-the-scenes power on Capitol Hill. These people tend to be young and highly intelligent. They tend to have a bias against private institutions – especially big ones, and prefer to believe in the ability of big government to solve social and economic problems. Many staff members have never been exposed to life outside government or academia, and few have had any business experience. In addition, many staff members believe – with some justification – that they know more about the issues that the congressman or senator they work for. As a result, they often make important decisions, which the boss dutifully follows.

Finally, staff members have a special and symbiotic relationship with the press. The journalist depends on the staff member for the titbits of information needed to write a story. The staff member, in turn, depends upon the journalist for the kind of favourable coverage that either makes his boss look good, advances the staff member's political philosophy, or furthers his own career aspirations.

But while staff members are important, the single most effective way to get your issue across is through a personal visit to a legislator. The leader of your organization – the person with actual line responsibilities – should come in person, rather than your Washington representative or your public-relations executive.

Your chief executive officer will make the biggest impact because he will have the most credibility. After all, he has made the trip to Capitol Hill out of sincere conviction and experience. Public-relations people, by contrast, are often looked upon with suspicion in official Washington, in part for the reasons we've already seen – their bias seems too obvious, and their salaries too handsome – and in part because they usually don't have as much information as the people they represent.

How do you get an appointment with a senator or congressman? If you know him personally, call his office yourself and somebody there will get back to you. If you don't know him personally, find somebody who does, and ask that person to set up the appointment. If the go-between is another congressman, so much the better; this sort of arrangement goes on all the time. Or, if you've had any contact with a staff member, he or she may be able to help you. While all of these personal contacts will make it easier to see a legislator, even a complete stranger – assuming he represents a real constituency – can usually get an appointment if he's persistent and polite.

Once the appointment has been arranged, it's a good idea to research at least some of the following questions about the person you're going to be seeing: What is his voting record? Who are his major contributors? What committees does he sit on? What are the important economic ingredients in his district? What kind of coalition was responsible for his election, and what was his winning margin? Is his seat considered safe or marginal? What are his favourite causes and issues? Is he likely to face a primary battle in the next election? Is he beholden to any groups or individuals? Who is known to have an influence on him? Is he considered a leader, a follower, or an independent? Does he aspire to higher office?

Keep in mind that most congressmen are running scared. Before taking action or making any decisions, they have to weigh a whole complex of conflicting pressures and consequences. The more you understand these conflicts and consequences, the more convincing your presentation will be.

After you've completed the research, but before the actual meeting, you might send the legislator a packet of literature – especially favourable articles or editorials about your issue. But don't assume he will read your material before the meeting. Ideally, it will find its way to the appropriate staff person, and if you're lucky, maybe he will read it.

Assume that your meeting time will be limited, and decide in advance what major points you want to make. Rehearse your presentation by having somebody listen to you and ask you tough questions.

On the day of your appointment, arrive early. A legislator's schedule is subject to wide fluctuations, and you might be called a few minutes early. By the same token, you might be asked to wait an hour because he's tied up in a committee meeting. Or worse, your meeting might be interrupted or even concluded in the middle because your host has to appear for a floor vote. Remember: your agenda may be *your* only concern, but for the legislator it's one of several dozen issues he's trying to balance.

Once the meeting is actually under way, make your points carefully and simply. Tell the legislator that he should feel free to interrupt you at any time with his questions. When he does interrupt, answer his questions and then gently guide the conversation back to the topic at hand.

Stick to the facts, and don't guess or speculate. If you inadvertently mislead him on any point, correct it later in a letter. Be brief; the less time you take up, the more your visit will be appreciated. Give the legislator as much time and information as he wants, but don't impose yourself. Stay away from long-winded speeches and shaggy-dog stories.

During the meeting, you may want to give the legislator a one-page summary of your main points. When the meeting ends, offer more detailed material for him or his staff person. Try to meet with the appropriate staff person immediately afterwards or at some future time to discuss the situation in more detail.

When you get back to your office, write a short letter to the legislator thanking him for the meeting. This is strictly a courtesy and is *not* an appropriate time to make new arguments or to repeat old ones.

Many years ago, I learned that a fundamental rule of politics is that you shouldn't waste your time and energy on people who are fundamentally opposed to your position. At the same time, there are occasions when it makes sense to seek a meeting with a legislator who seems to oppose the cause you believe in. For one thing, debating an opponent will sharpen your arguments. The more familiar you become with the questions and arguments raised by the other side, the more effectively you can make your case. Another possibility is that your presumed opponent has concerns that you didn't know about, and for which you can provide real and reassuring answers. Finally, your opponent will come to see you as a real person, and he will emerge with a better understanding of your position. (Both of these factors will pay off if and when a compromise has to be worked out down the road.) In addition, your meeting will pay an unexpected dividend when it comes to discussing other issues in the future – when you may find yourself on the same side of the fence.

Although the personal meeting with a legislator is your best bet, there are other ways to get support and attention for your position on Capitol Hill. You might try to get at least one supporter legislator to sign a letter and then circulate it to his colleagues. This gesture will be noticed by his fellow congressmen or senators, and will probably generate some press coverage as well.

Another technique is to ask a friendly legislator to insert one of your statements into the *Congressional Record*. Believe it or not, there are people in Washington (and elsewhere) who actually read this publication. But far more important is that you can then photocopy the statement and use it for your own purposes: the distinctive typeface of the *Congressional Record* will add a measure of credibility to your position.

Another possibility is to ask for the opportunity to write a speech for one of the legislators supporting your position. To prevent problems over turf, this offer should always be made through the appropriate staff member.

Still another way to reach legislators is through their hometown newspapers, in full view of the people who put them into office. Especially in the House of Representatives, the major national papers represent only part of the story; in many cases, it's the hometown press that really counts. These, after all, are the papers that are constituents are reading, and it is in these communities that the next election battle will be fought.

One way to get your story into the hometown papers is to buy the space and write your own copy. During the week of July 9, 1973, when gasoline shortages were a major national concern, Mobil took out ads in the hometown newspapers of all members of Congress. Entitled 'An open letter on the gasoline shortage,' the document was addressed to the appropriate congressman, and began with these words:

> We are publishing this letter in your hometown newspaper, and in those of the other Members of Congress, because we want you

> and your constituents to have the facts about the gasoline shortage as we see them. We are doing this because many people are being misled by the absolute nonsense, totally unsupported charges, and outright lies being spread around by a variety of people.

In the paragraphs that followed, we were able to respond with hard, factual evidence to contradict the rampant rumours and myths about the petrol shortage.

This brings us to the topic of politicians and money. Half a century ago, there was a prominent Brooklyn politician by the name of Hymie Shorenstein. Although it was widely believed that Hymie could neither read nor write, he was the county clerk of Brooklyn and a powerful figure in local politics.

In 1936, a few weeks before the election, Hymie selected a certain lawyer to run for judge. As the election drew close, the lawyer came to Hymie and said: 'Listen, there's nothing going on in my campaign. No posters, no parades, no leaflets, nothing.'

'Come with me,' said Hymie. 'I want to show you something.'

Hymie took the candidate down to see the Staten Island ferry. As the boat came in, Hymie turned to him and said: 'You see the ferry? Think of that ferry as President Roosevelt. Now, do you see all the garbage that ferry is dragging in with it? That garbage is you! So go home and stop worrying!'

For better or worse, there are no longer any ferries in American politics. For that matter, there are no Hymie Shorenstein's either. The biggest single change in American politics in recent years is the declining importance of the major parties. And for holders of public office, this boils down to one unpleasant fact: increasingly, each candidate now has to raise his own campaign funds.

Should you participate in this process? Should your corporate PAC channel money to political campaigns? Yes, by all means – so long as you do so with your eyes open and with no illusions.

And so long as you understand that your PAC contribution will have no effect on the candidate's political behaviour. While it may be hard to believe that a group that supports a legislator isn't going to be well thought of, the practical solution is that the interests of contributors are so diverse that their contributions often cancel each other out. Besides, the legal limitations are so strict that in the final analysis these gifts usually don't mean very much. And despite what Common Cause and other organizations would have

An open letter on the gasoline shortage to:

Senator:
John Doe

Representative:
Richard Roe

We are publishing this letter in your home town newspaper, and in those of the other Members of Congress, because we want you and your constituents to have the facts about the gasoline shortage as we see them. We are doing this because many people are being misled by the absolute nonsense, totally unsupported charges, and outright lies being spread around by a variety of people. For example:

"There are sufficient supplies available to the oil industry so that there need be no serious shortage of gasoline or any other petroleum product for any purpose in this nation."

"But the fact is, much of the so-called energy crisis is being concocted in the board rooms and public relations offices of the nation's major oil companies."

"I suggest that circumstantial evidence supports the conclusion that the major oil companies are using the fuel shortage they helped create to drive out their competition."

What these and other such statements boil down to is a series of charges that the shortage is contrived. That it is a hoax perpetrated by oil companies to raise prices and drive unbranded marketers out of business. That it is a massive conspiracy, a price gouge to end all price gouges.

Not one of these charges is true. All are based on misinformation. Some are outright lies. Here are the facts:

I. Gasoline production is at an all-time high

When they hear the word "shortage," many people think the industry must be supplying *less* than before. Far from it.

The U.S. oil industry is making *more* gasoline than ever before – 5% more than last year. That translates into an increase of 13,700,000 gallons a day above 1972 – *which would have been more than enough to meet the demand growth of almost any previous year in history.* The problem is that with gasoline production up 5% over last year, demand is up about 6.2%. The shortages, which may come and go due to temporary swings in demand and supply, have shown up in the fact that some service stations occasionally run out of gasoline, and many dealers have chosen to operate on shorter hours and to close on Sundays.

II. Political decisions have produced the shortage

The following factors, all essentially resulting from political decisions, have produced today's shortage:

(1) While potentially large oil reserves are believed to lie off the U.S. East and West Coasts – our most promising oil province, since the onshore U.S. has been more heavily drilled-up than any other part of the world – these offshore areas are barred to exploration, and U.S. crude production is dropping. Oil companies had no control over this.

(2) Over five years after the largest oil field ever discovered in North America was found on the North Slope of Alaska, construction of a pipeline to bring this oil to market is still stalled. Oil companies had no control over this.

(3) The United States is short of refining capacity, and will be critically short in a year or two, as a result of erratic government import policies, environmental constraints, and inability to bring the largest, most economical tankers into U.S. ports. Oil companies had no control over this.

(4) In terms of volumes, demand for gasoline is growing well over twice as much as it did during the 1960s, with pollution-control equipment and convenience devices such as air-conditioners accounting for a large part of this year's increase. Oil companies had no control over this.

(5) The shortage of natural gas caused by ill-advised government regulatory policies has forced industrial users to use large quantities of heating oil, which has caused a shortage of that product for the consumer. Oil companies had no control over this.

(6) Two of the major oil-exporting countries in the Middle East and North Africa have reduced crude oil production. Oil companies had no control over this.

(7) Price controls are impeding the importation of higher-priced oil products into our country. Oil companies had no control over this.

III. Is there a conspiracy? Is the shortage contrived?

If there was ever an industry in which it would be impossible to conspire, it's oil. Conspiracy requires secrecy. If you stop to think of all the bodies of government – in every branch of government, at every level – that have long involved themselves in our business, you'll realize we couldn't conspire if we wanted to. We operate in a fishbowl.

Dozens of agencies of the federal government, a horde of Congressional committees, and agencies of the 50 states and various municipalities regulate, investigate, or monitor the oil industry's activities.

Further, oil companies – even the largest ones – are so widely divergent in their size, their interests, their needs, their opportunities, and their views that it would be impossible to put a conspiracy together. Oil is one of the least-concentrated major industries in the world. No oil company supplies as much as 9% of the U.S. gasoline market.

IV. The "independent" marketers

You have doubtless seen charges that "the major oil companies" are cutting off gasoline supplies to non-major-brand ("independent") marketers to drive them out of business.

You should know that the overwhelming majority of service station dealers in this country are independent businessmen, whether they sell under the Mobil brand name or the brand of one of our major competitors or under their own private brand. All these dealers set their own retail prices, their working conditions, and usually their hours of operation.

Many non-major-brand marketers have in the past chosen to rely on day-to-day purchases of gasoline from oil companies instead of entering into long-term supply arrangements. This policy worked to their advantage as long as supplies were adequate, and especially when there were surpluses. Now that the surplus has disappeared, they are having difficulty obtaining gasoline.

As for Mobil, we have established an allocation system to ensure fair treatment of our customers. We believe this system will enable us to supply these customers at least as much gasoline and other refined products this year as last year.

V. Where do we go from here?

It's going to take several years to remedy the situation. A pipeline has to be built to move the oil discovered over five years ago on the North Slope of Alaska. The outer continental shelf off the U.S. East and West Coasts has to be opened to exploration for new reserves of oil and natural gas. Superports have to be built. Oil companies must be enabled to obtain satisfactory sites for new refineries. Massive research and development programs have to be undertaken to make the production of non-conventional oil and gas from oil shale and coal economically feasible and environmentally safe. Construction of nuclear power plants to generate electricity must be accelerated. All of these require long lead times, and they can't be accomplished by the oil industry alone.

This is why Mobil has been running newspaper ads across the country, and doing a good many other things, to urge people to conserve gasoline and to use all energy more efficiently. As a further step in this direction, we have totally eliminated our gasoline advertising and are focusing our efforts on providing greater public information on how our country can tackle its energy problems rationally and equitably.

VI. Why this letter

Our intention is not to get into a posture of charges and counter-charges, but rather to accomplish two things:

(1) To set the record straight on the gasoline shortage and to put the lie to the charge of conspiracy, to help people understand the shortage is real and will be with us for some while, and to suggest practical ways to cope with it.

(2) To try to elicit from you and your constituents a national effort, such as our country has not seen since World War II, to use wisely the energy resources available to us and to establish new policies to alleviate energy problems in the years just ahead.

Mobil®

you believe, contributions from political-action committees and other sources don't influence legislation. The legislator's vote is invariably determined by some combination of his conscience and his constituents; and not by your relatively small donation.

So why give money at all? There are two reasons. First, because you're philosophically in tune with the legislator and you want to support him. And second, because while your contribution won't gain you any great advantage, you might keep in mind the punch line in this classic Jewish joke:

> A great actor in the Yiddish theatre dies onstage.
> 'Give him an enema!' cries a lady in the balcony.
> 'Lady, he's *dead*,' shouts the manager. 'It wouldn't help.'
> 'Maybe not,' she replies, 'but it vouldn't *hoit*!'

The easiest way to contribute to a political campaign is through a political-action committee. Again, don't expect anything in return for your contribution. Similarly, don't channel PAC money into the campaign of a candidate you disagreed with in the hope that your gift will help him change his mind. It won't.

If you're going to make a PAC contribution, it's generally better to do so directly and independently rather than through a fund-raising event. The only reason to make your contribution together with other people's is that the event itself may be worth attending because of the contacts you can make.

Another way to channel money to a legislator is by inviting him to speak to your organization. By paying an honorarium, you are helping the congressman or senator survive in an underpaid profession. At the same time, you are educating and motivating your members or employees. By the same token, you are exposing the legislator to the concerns and issues of your group.

Another technique is to commission the legislator to write an article for your publication, for which he will be appropriately paid. In addition to supporting his campaign, you are helping the legislator disseminate his views.

CONGRESSIONAL HEARINGS

Congressional hearings (also known as committee hearings and public hearings) are yet another way to focus the attention of the Washington public on your issue. Officially, there are two kinds of hearings: legislative and oversight. Oversight hearings are held to reexamine the administration of existing legislation. Legislative hearings, which are far more common, are held to consider bills that have been referred to various congressional and Senate committees and subcommittees for further deliberation.

That, at least, is how the system is supposed to work. But hearings are often held for reasons that have little to do with either oversight or legislation. For example, a hearing may be held to underscore support for (or opposition to) the administration's viewpoint on a particular issue. Or to generate public or press opinion on a particular issue. Hearings are also held to embarrass or punish individuals or institutions. In 1973, for example, Senator Henry Jackson held hearings on energy whose real purpose was to manipulate the press against the oil industry, and to shift the blame for the energy crisis from Congress to the oil companies.

From time to time, hearings are held to give an important constituent group the satisfaction of knowing that they have had the opportunity to make their case before an arm of Congress. Or to provide a grandstand forum for making political or career-enhancing statements. Or, in the case of hearings that are held in a member's home district, to enhance the prestige of that legislator.

With respect to congressional hearings, the majority and minority members may have very different goals in mind. The majority party generally decides whether there will be a hearing in the first place; it is they who structure the hearing and control both the list of witnesses and the order in which they will speak. What comes out of a hearing is usually heavily skewed to what the majority side wants.

If you're going to be dealt with favourably in a hearing, you'll generally know this in advance because the committee staff has already been in touch with you to discuss your testimony. Treat the hearing like any friendly interview situation. You will be asked to draft a statement for the record, which will probably be read aloud. In addition, you should provide the staff with a list of questions you would like to be asked, as well as a list of points you expect the other side to make – together with your responses to these points.

After you've testified, even if it's been all sweetness and light and the minority hasn't laid a glove on you, you're still not out of the woods. The press may want to interview you, and their questions may well be different – and tougher – than those you were asked during the hearing. If subsequent witnesses have disputed either your facts or your conclusions, the press will try to exploit that discrepancy in their questions. The press reports of the hearings are usually far more important than the actual testimony, so prepare yourself well to deal with reporters. At the very least, you should examine the prepared testimony of other witnesses and be prepared to comment on their statements.

If you expect that you will be dealt with unfavourably, or if it appears that the hearing has been constructed to embarrass you or your cause, you might consider convening a small group of reporters the day before the hearing for a frank discussion of your point of view. But do this only if you're fully prepared to answer all of their questions. If you hold this meeting early enough, the press reports could come out before the hearing, which could be to your advantage, because in any debate, the side that goes first enjoys the advantage of seeming to set the agenda.

Because even favourable hearings can be stressful, let's consider a few ways to put your best foot forward. First, never go to a hearing alone. Always bring two or three people with you, even if they're not going to say anything. It helps if they look important and carrying bulging briefcases. They could be people from top management, or a prominent law professor, or outside counsel. Make a point of introducing them to the committee at the start of your testimony.

Second, it's a good idea to bring along a press-relations person who can readily identify various journalists and quickly assess their relative importance. This person can facilitate interviews and should help you to interact with the press in an orderly and professional manner.

Third, in your dress and demeanour, try to project an air of self-confidence. You don't want to appear arrogant or disdainful, but you want to create the impression that you know more about this issue than anyone else in the room.

Fourth, you must rehearse. Hearings are intimidating, so try to anticipate every question that can be thrown at you. Have your colleagues fire tough questions at you, and give yourself time to practise giving the answers. Even if you're confident that you know the answers, practise saying them. You are, after all, an amateur at this, and you're going up against seasoned professionals. Even experienced actors go through a dress rehearsal; you owe it to yourself to have a *stress* rehearsal. Once you've been through this process, your self-confidence goes through the roof.

Finally, if you can afford it, bring your own television crew into the hearing room to film the entire proceedings. If commercial television stations are allowed to send cameras, your own crew cannot be kept out. This simple procedure does more than document the session; it also helps to keep the media honest. If you can't afford a camera crew, be sure to make an audio tape.

THE WASHINGTON PRESS CORPS

Washington is teeming with reporters. On a per capita basis, there are more journalists in Washington than anywhere else in the country – if not the world. The total number, including free-lancers and the foreign press, is estimated to be as high as ten thousand.

The world that these ten thousand people live in is highly specialized, and consists of legislators and their staffs, bureaucrats, diplomats, lobbyists, and – above all – other reporters. It's not surprising, then, that Washington reporters are generally out of touch with the rest of American society. The problem has grown so serious that even the reporters themselves now acknowledge it. In his recent study on the Washington press corps, Stephen Hess of the Brookings Institution asked journalists if they felt that reporters often miss how government affects people 'out there.' An astounding 82 per cent of the journalists agreed, and more than half thought the problem was serious.

Among Hess's other findings: one-third of the Washington journalists were graduated from the country's top colleges and universities; half of the Washington press corps have never taken a single college-level course in journalism; and almost half – 48 per cent – believe that political reporting suffers from a liberal bias.

Because so many reporters are chasing so few stories, there is, naturally, a high degree of competition among the Washington journalists – even among reporters who serve totally different publics. This competitive environment is best symbolized by the long-standing battle between the *Washington Post* and the *New York Times*. Every night, within minutes of publication, the *Post* and the *Times* each receive via wire photo a front page of the competition's early edition, an arrangement that allows both papers to see if they've missed a major story and to rectify the situation in the final morning edition. During its Watergate coverage, the *Post* would routinely delay its most important stories until the final edition to prevent the *Times* from stealing its stories. So much for the public's paramount right to know.

In Washington, people in positions of power and influence actively court the press and try to use it. This is in sharp contrast to business and political leaders everywhere else, most of whom go to great lengths to avoid the press. There are several reasons for this close relationship. For one thing, politicians need the press at least as much as the press needs them. Almost everyone in town is concerned with making public policy and trying to sell it, or with advancing somebody's political career, or with running for reelection. All of these efforts are impossible without the press.

For another thing, people in Washington have learned a very important lesson about the news, a lesson that often escapes their counterparts in other cities: the news is always skewed towards those who are most willing to talk.

Finally, because information is the local currency, reporters routinely buy their information with other information. 'The press knows everything,' Joan Mondale once said. 'You learn so much from talking to them.'

It's not surprising, then, that more gossip is generated in Washington than just about anywhere else. And when this gossip deals with high-level personalities, the resulting story can often pass for news. A staple of Washington gossip-as-journalism is the generic story about the feud among members of the White House staff – or any other powerful group, for that matter: Who's up? Who's down? Whose star is rising or falling? Who's got the president's ear? Whose policy is prevailing this time? To read some press reports, you would think that major policy decisions are merely a function of which adviser got to see the president the day before yesterday – a phenomenon that the *New Republic* recently called 'the curse of aides.'

Another fact you should be aware of is that reporters and people in government – especially staff members – tend to have a very close relationship, to the point that journalists will sometimes prompt government people to begin an investigation so that they, the journalists, will have a story to report.

For all their excited talk about 'investigative journalism,' the fact is that reporters are rarely powerful enough to conduct a real investigation. More often, they turn to those who do have that power – the staff members of the congressional committees. The staffers leak information for their own purposes, and the journalists dutifully print it.

As a consequence of this peculiar relationship, news sources are to Washington journalism as informers are to the police. Because the Washington press depends on leaks, anonymous sources, and stolen documents, reporters are often willing to offer their sources protection and immunity from journalistic prosecution. Journalists have been known to recommend people for jobs in government simply because these people are potentially good sources. They have been known to ask people in positions of power to subpoena material that they want for a story. And they have been known to threaten to use a particular story unless the source comes up with a better one.

In other cities, reporters cover celebrities. In Washington, reporters are themselves celebrities, to the point that no first-class dinner party is complete without a couple of prominent journalists. This situation exists not only because political figures need the press so urgently, but also because Washington, being a provincial capital, has an acute shortage of intellectuals, novelists, playwrights, critics, and artists. With so little competition, the journalists win by default.

Washington reporters enjoy some very special privileges. They receive advance copies of government speeches and announcements. They are often shown secret documents. They have special areas set aside for them in all important government buildings. The government spends a great deal of time and money to make their jobs easier. As a result, the journalists often have better access to a public figure than that person's own colleagues and subordinates.

At the same time, reporters are definitely on the outside looking in. In Washington, even more than in other cities, journalists are voyeurs. A veteran editor once quipped that the job of a Washington reporter is to sit around in the halls, waiting for the grown-ups to tell them what's going on. This situation, quite naturally, breeds frustration in reporters. One result is that a journalist may begin to view himself as a participant rather than an observer, and – often unconsciously – may attempt to create policy through his reporting.

Another result of this continuing frustration is that journalism in Washington has – even by the standards of the profession – a high degree of destructiveness. The most coveted Washington stories, in descending order of importance, are: any report of wrongdoing or illegality; personal hanky-panky that borders on illegality or impropriety; advance information on policy initiatives – or on almost anything else; conflicts among high public officials, especially if one principal is quoted talking about another.

This is especially true at the *Washington Post*. After Bob Woodward was promoted to metro editor of the *Post* in 1979, he told his 104 editors and reporters that he wanted 'holy shit!' stories. Watergate was the *Post*'s founding myth, and many of the paper's efforts since that time have been attempts to duplicate that success.

The newsroom at the *Post* is a pressure cooker. There is a tremendous amount of competition among the younger reporters to produce hot stories, a situation that gave rise to Janet Cooke's fabricated story of 'Jimmy,' the child heroin addict. It's unfortunate, but a *Post* reporter is more likely than his counterparts from other papers to be looking for a story that involves wrongdoing, internal strife, or gossip.

The Washington bureau of the *Wall Street Journal* is more likely to be interested in the business side of Washington: the SEC, energy, finance, and the Federal Reserve. But the back page of the *Journal* pays close attention to the political world of Washington.

The *New York Times* reporter is more inclined to get the real story, even if it isn't very glamourous. The *Times* claims to be the nation's paper of record, and its editors make a genuine effort to deliver on that promise. Theirs is a more mature institution than the *Post*, by which I mean that they take their public responsibilities more seriously. Their business section is first-rate, and so is their coverage of economic and cultural affairs. The *Post*, by contrast, appears to be less interested in subjects outside of politics and personalities.

Both the *Post* and the *Times* feature excellent political columnists, who inhabit a world that is separate from the reporters. And because many of these columnists are syndicated, their influence can be considerable. David Broder of the *Post* is generally acknowledged as the nation's most influential political columnist. James Reston of the *Times* has been a powerful figure for three decades, and while his influence is waning, he is still important. Other significant columnists in Washington include George Will, William Safire, James Kilpatrick, Jack Germond and Jules Witcover, Mary McGrory, Ben Wattenberg, Carl Rowan, and Art Buchwald.

One level down are the guest columnists who appear with some regularity on the op-ed pages of the *Times* and the *Post*, such as Alan Greenspan, Lester Thurow, Gar Alpowitz, Clark Clifford, and Paul Nitze.

Whenever there's a crowd waiting to get in the front door, the smart operator goes around to the back. Keep in mind that not all print journalism dealing with Washington appears in the *Times*, the *Post* or the *Journal*. Very often a story is broken by an enterprising reporter in the Washington bureau of an out-of-town paper. Among the more important papers, in terms of visibility in Washington – at least among the press corps – are the *Los Angeles Times*, the *Baltimore Sun*, the *Boston Globe*, the *Christian Science Monitor*, the *Chicago Tribune*, the *Atlanta Constitution* and the *Atlanta Journal*, the *New York Daily News*, the *Philadelphia Inquirer*, the *Miami Herald*, and the *Detroit Free Press*. Other papers of at least minor importance include the *Louisville Courier-Journal*, the *Saint Louis Post-Dispatch*, the *Cleveland Plain Dealer*, the *Hartford Courant*, and Long Island's *Newsday*.

While these papers are not widely read by official Washington, they are followed closely by two important groups: legislators reading their hometown press, and journalists trying to keep up with the competition, who may take one of these stories and run with it.

On the surface, that's the end of the list. But in Washington decision making is highly complex. There are so many different centres of power, and so many sources of information, that decision makers are constantly bombarded by people who want to press a particular point of view, or by literature that professes to have all the answers.

If you're going to compete in this environment, you have no choice but to cover every base you can. Staff people on Capitol Hill, in the White House, and with the various regulatory agencies tend to be voracious readers of materials issued by the reporting services. Although these publications are generally overlooked by journalists, they often contain useful and specialized information. These publications are like vacuum cleaners, as they swoop up information on particular subjects. They are respected as accurate, neutral, and nonphilosophical.

Such publications are useful in two ways. First, if you have information to disseminate, this may be the place to send it. At the same time, these publications can be a valuable source of overt intelligence – especially for a company that can't afford to hire expensive Washington talent to gather information.

The Bureau of National Affairs (a private organization, despite its official-sounding name) alone publishes more than fifty newsletters. Prentice Hall and Commerce Clearing House also publish newsletters. These publications are subscribed to by various industries and specialized segments of the public. They cover legislation, regulatory agencies, and cabinet offices, and almost no detail is too small for them to notice.

Similarly, you should be aware of Washington's wide variety of special-interest groups and their newsletters. These include such diverse publications and organizations as *Congressional Watch* (the Nader publication), Common Cause, the Media Institute Forum, *Privacy Journal*, Accuracy in Media, and *Near East Report* (the Israel lobby). These are part of the enormous stream of substantive publications that swirl around Washington, competing for the attention of the press and policymakers alike.

Finally, there is the Washington trade press. These publications provide insider information, gossip, and general news of the industries they represent. They also cover issues involving legislation and regulations. There are hundreds of trade papers, and they are so important in Washington that some officials actually read them to find out what's going on in their own department. Many 'inside' stories appearing in the general press have originated in these specialized publications. There are far too many of these to list them all, but here is a sample of some that are closely followed in Washington (although some are published elsewhere): *Education Daily* and *Higher Education Daily; Oilgram, Petroleum Intelligence Weekly, Oil Daily and Gas Journal; Sludge* (waste disposal); *Automotive News; Nucleonics Week* (energy); *American Medical News, Medical World News, Washington Report on Medicine and Health*, and *Blue Sheet* (health); *Aviation Week and Space Technology, Armed Forces Journal, Astronautics and Aeronautics, Air Force Magazine*, and *U.S Naval Proceedings*.

No matter which publication you end up approaching, it's best to be aware of the ways that news originates in Washington. The primary source is events, which include speeches, congressional hearings, press conferences, and demonstrations. The second source of news in Washington involves leaks to the press, which generally serve the purpose of the person providing the information. It's very difficult for a journalist to ignore a leak, in part because it's so flattering to be offered one. The appeal of the leak to the person providing information is not only the obvious one, that he is able to get his side of the story across; it's also that leaks constitute a virtual guarantee of benign treatment on the part of the reporter who accepted the favour. When he held public office, Henry Kissinger was a master at this arrangement.

The third source of news entails 'enterprise' stories, in which the reporter himself (or his editor) generates the idea. These stories are the least common, and many stories that appear to originate this way really belong in the previous category. Although journalists don't like to admit it, most of them react far more often than they initiate.

Now, let's examine some specific ways to general press coverage and media exposure, or both, in Washington.

First, Washington radio and television stations have an abundance of talk shows, most of which attract a good-sized audience. On some of these, you're simply interviewed by the host; on others, you may be asked to debate somebody who holds a different position, or to answer questions phoned in by listeners. If you're willing to spend several days at it, you can end up with quite a bit of airtime. Keep in mind that the people who produce talk shows need you just as much as you need them. They're constantly searching for new issues and fresh material, so even if you or your organization are small and relatively unknown, this free and abundantly available opportunity is one you must consider.

Another structured situation that will generate press coverage and enlist supporters is giving a speech. A number of organizations in Washington provide regular forums for lectures and debates. The National Press Club is ideal because its events are always well covered. But don't rule out church and synagogue groups, colleges and universities, and political organizations. If you give a speech in a relatively modest setting, be sure to invite the press, and to provide any reporters who do not show up with either the text of your remarks or a one-page summary.

You can take speech making one step further by staging a debate. People or groups with unpopular causes often have real difficulties in getting the attention of the media. Debates are an excellent way to correct that imbalance, as they attract far more interest – and generally more media coverage – that a regular speech. Debates always carry the potential for conflict and dramatic confrontation, so they're an ideal way to get your issue across, either in person or through the media.

On the other hand, not every opportunity for exposure will arise in such a structured way. You will often have the chance to talk to government officials, reporters, and other important people at benefits, cocktail parties, or salons. In these settings, forget the code of conduct that may be operative back home. Remember: in Washington, you're not violating any rules of etiquette by talking business with the fellow across the table at a dinner party. That's what he's there for.

Finally, you might consider attracting press and other public attention by holding a demonstration. To date, this very effective tactic has been used to best advantage by the left, the farmers, and some portions of the new right. But what about the business community? I've long thought there ought to be a businessman's march on Washington. Imagine: a hundred thousand business men and women would march through the streets of the city in gray flannel suits. In their arms would be every government form they have been required to file. After the march, this great mass of people would converge at the Federal Trade Commission and burn all of their papers. They would then move on to the Securities and Exchange Commission for an all-night candlelight vigil.

Because television is such a willing handmaiden, demonstrations are a wonderful way to get your issue covered. The Naders of this world are pros at this technique, and it's high time the rest of us took a page from their book.

BUILDING COALITIONS WITH PRIVATE POWER CENTRES

Because we live in an era of coalition politics, it's imperative to identify other individuals and groups who will stand with you on your issue. Look for people and groups and who are similarly situated, who have the most to gain from your success and the most to lose from your failure. You might even develop a formal coalition and call a press conference to show how broadly based your alliances really are.

The less likely your allies, the more interesting and newsworthy your coalition becomes. Mobil once joined with the Sierra Club in a fight to get the television networks to run our issue ads without censorship. The Sierra Club wanted the same right, although of course the substance of their ads would have been very different. This unusual coalition made for some great media coverage, and was good for both sides. (Unfortunately, it wasn't good enough to get the network executives to change their minds – and they still haven't.)

Below are some of the key private-sector power centres in Washington. For the most part, they're a combination of shadow government organizations and narrowly-focused special-interest groups, all working to produce reports, studies, and position papers. On almost any issue, at least a couple of these groups will be active on one side, or the other.

Labour Unions. The AFL-CIO and many of the large unions have their national headquarters in Washington. On their staffs are a significant number of very intelligent and high effective lobbyists. Incidentally, it was the labour unions who organized the first PAC, so these people are old pros on Capitol Hill. If your interest coincides with theirs, you've got a powerful ally.

General Trade Associations. There are three major groups that serve business as a whole. The United States Chamber of Commerce is a collection of many large and small businesses. It produces its own television shows, and is extremely active on the Hill, especially when it comes to issues involving regulation.

The National Association of Manufacturers is exactly what the name implies; NAM's chief interest is economic expansion. The third group, the Business Roundtable, is composed of the CEO's of the large blue-chip corporations. It takes positions on specific legislation, and because it is thought to speak for corporate America, its voice is quite effective.

Specific Trade Organizations. Virtually every industry in America has a trade association with a Washington headquarters, and there are offices to represent everything from milk producers to hat makers. Almost all of them have lobbyists and publish reports and newsletters. These groups act as a countervailing force to the so-called public-interest groups.

Think Tanks. In recent years, the party that has been voted out of office has retreated to think tanks. When Jimmy Carter won in 1976, the Republicans withdrew to the Center for Strategic and International Studies at Georgetown University, the American Enterprise Institute, and the Heritage Foundation. With the Reagan victory in 1980, the Democrats formed the Democracy Project, the National Policy Exchange, the Center for National Policy, and the Roosevelt Center for American Policy Studies. Members of both parties have found haven at such mainstream places as the Brookings Institution, the Woodrow Wilson Center at the Smithsonian Institution, and the Kennedy School of Government at Harvard. Now more than ever, the Washington think tanks constitute the leisure of the theory class.

The National Democratic and Republican Committees. These groups have less power every year, but they're still influential. Although party discipline means less than ever before, the national committees still have a fairly good idea of what the party faithful believe in, so their support is worth seeing.

Special-Interest Groups. There are far too many to mention, but these include the Sierra Club, the National Audubon Society, the Media Institute, Common Cause, Accuracy in Media, and so on. With the exception of Common Cause, which is well endowed, most of these groups are very good at getting their viewpoints across despite a small budget. They regularly publish reports that generate press coverage. Their representatives are always ready to go on television and radio. The most successful of all the special-interest groups has been the complex of 'public-interest' organizations founded by Ralph Nader and his disciples.

Washington Law Firms. There are three kinds of law firms in Washington. First, there are those that practice law in ways that are similar to law firms in any other city. This group is of no immediate concern. Second, there are the specialized law firms, which are composed of lawyers who concentrate in particular legal areas. They often appear before regulatory agencies on behalf of large corporations, trade associations, or labour unions. In many cases, these lawyers have previously served on the staffs of the agencies they now appear before – a situation that has generated considerable debate (and some legislation) as to its propriety. If you require this kind of representation, research the appropriate firms to find the kinds of expertise you really need.

The third type of Washington law firm doesn't really practise law at all. What it provides is representation – lobbying, contacts with legislators, and the like. The lawyers in these firms are really more like consultants, and they routinely advise their clients as to the political climate and the political implications of a given issue. Included in this group are the 'superlawyers' who move easily between government and the private sector – such as Clark Clifford, William Fulbright, Joseph Califano, and, more recently, Walter Mondale.

Public-Relations Firms. Most Washington public-relations firms are similar to the third group of lawyers. But they provide one important additional ingredient: they can help you in dealing with the press. The size of the firm doesn't matter; what counts is the reputation of the person who will be assigned to you. And remember, in Washington reputation has a lot to do with fame and mystique.

Among Washington's premier practitioners of public relations is Timmons and Company, composed of former Republican White House officials, including Tom Korologos. Being represented by somebody like Timmons and Company gives you an automatic special status that is real but hard to define. But be careful: high-level representation can also work against you. By going over their heads, you may provoke the resentment of the middle managers, and very often they're the ones who actually get things done.

THE NATIONAL TOWN MEETING

One day back in 1974, I heard from Fred Dutton, an old friend who had served as cabinet secretary in the Kennedy administration. Fred suggested that we at Mobil might want to sponsor a series of open forums on contemporary issues that would be held at the Kennedy Center in Washington. We would provide the funding and the publicity, while Dutton would select the issues and invite the speakers.

I agreed immediately, as this was an opportunity for us to assume a leadership role in the discussion of controversial issues. To sponsor a series of public debates in the nation's capital, where the discussions themselves would be newsworthy – this was too good an opportunity to pass up.

We called our project National Town Meeting, and the topics it covered ranged from death to taxes, including the Social Security system, capital punishment, the defence budget, the equal-rights amendment, and abortion. (To avoid any conflict of interest, there were no forums dealing with oil or energy policy.)

The format was always the same: two prominent guests would debate an important issue of public policy. The speakers might be government officials, leaders of constituent groups like Ralph Nader, Phyllis Schlafly, or Bella Abzug, or experts from academic institutions. At each National Town Meeting, the speakers began by having their say on the issue. Following their opening statements, they would be questioned by members of the press. Finally, the audience would join in with their own questions.

The meetings were held Wednesday mornings from 10:30 until noon. They were always free and open to the public, and were carried live on National Public Radio.

What were some of the gains we achieved with the National Town Meeting? First, we made an important, albeit subtle, point about the way issues could be discussed in a public setting. When the programme began in 1974, we at Mobil were having a great deal of trouble getting our point of view across. During and after the first energy crisis, nobody wanted to hear from the big oil companies; it was far easier to make them the scapegoats for what had happened to society and the national economy. As a result, we felt frustrated, shortchanged, and closed out of the marketplace of ideas.

In response, we were eager to provide a public forum that didn't depend on the filtration system of the press. Even though our particular issues would not be dealt with, we felt it was important to let all sides be heard on every issue. We were committed to an honest dialogue, and we hoped that this process would soon be extended to energy issues as well.

Second, by including prominent political officials, leaders of constituency groups, and members of the press, we reinforced among those key publics our commitment to debating the issues in a public and open manner.

Third, the National Town Meetings reinforced other efforts we were making to present ourselves as an intellectually respectable company – in sharp contrast to the public's view of the oil companies.

Fourth, the meetings often became news-making events in themselves, which in turn attracted favourable media attention for us, the sponsors.

Fifth, because National Town Meeting quickly became a

successful institution, we had a modest influence on the shaping of a national agenda.

Sixth, on a smaller level, the meetings provided an opportunity for our Washington people to meet a large and diverse group of opinion makers in a very favourable environment.

Finally, Mobil benefitted because of the posters that we produced for the event as well as our full-page ads in the newspapers.

EIGHT

Affinity-of-Purpose Marketing: The Case of *Masterpiece Theatre*

BEFORE WE TAKE A close look at *Masterpiece Theatre*, which is easily the most spectacular and successful project I've been involved in, let's take a few minutes to consider the broader issues it raises. On the one hand, virtually everbody who is familiar with *Masterpiece Theatre* agrees that it has been both a tremendous artistic success and a major contribution to American television – if not *the* major contribution. On the other hand, Mobil's involvement with *Masterpiece Theatre* raises a fundamental and challenging question: Why should a publicly owned company spend any of its energy and resources on television drama, no matter how good the shows may be?

After all, it could be argued, if the funds that we allocate to *Masterpiece Theatre* and other discretionary projects are not absolutely esential to the running of our business, that money should rightfully be distributed to our shareholders in the form of higher dividends. And if our shareholders choose to use that money to support culture and the arts, that should be their decision.

From where I sit, however, there are several good reasons for corporations to be involved in the arts and culture. The fundamental reason, which I outlined earlier in this book, is that free institutions in our society do not exist by divine right. Just as individual citizens have certain responsibilities in our democracy, corporate citizens have a commensurable responsibility to support and strengthen the society that permits us all to flourish. and one of the best ways for us to achieve that goal is by supporting the various nonprofit institutions that protect our various freedoms and enrich the quality of our lives. In other words, we support the arts because an institution like ours has an obligation to be involved.

Does this line of argument sound hopelessly naive? Some people think so. When they hear me talk this way around the office, even my own staff gets a little cynical. 'Come on, Herb,' they tell me. 'Nobody is going to believe *that*.' So for those people who see themselves as more pragmatic and hardheaded, let me suggest some more directly self-serving reasons for corporations to be active in supporting the arts and culture.

First, the cultural excellence generally suggests corporate excellence. Invariably, your support of first-rate programmes in the arts and culture will significantly enhance the image of your company. If you undertake enough of these projects, and you execute them well, you can, over time, convey the idea that your corporation is associated only with excellence.

Second, these discretionary projects offer the opportunity to present your top management not as narrow-minded experts, but rather as corporate statesmen whose concerns go beyond the bottom line. In their new and expanded roles, your chairman and president will be seen as broad-based and far-reaching in their concerns – and intellectually entitled to be listened to on vital public-policy issues.

Third, arts and culture programmes enhance the pride of your employees. When a corporation is involved in a worthy project, its employees enjoy an added respect in their community and among their peers. As a result, whatever positive feelings they have towards the company will be reinforced.

Fourth, your company's involvement in the arts provides an excellent opportunity for leadership in your community. In a large city like New York or Los Angeles, being noticed may require your undertaking a fairly major project. In a smaller community, however, even a relatively modest programme will identify your company as a leader. Moreover, it's no secret that those individuals and institutions who actively support civic activities usually find themselves in a position to play an influential role in the community's political affairs.

Fifth, the sponsorship of cultural events allows you to entertain important customers at openings, special tours and similar events, where you have the opportunity to introduce important people to other important people. Business entertaining is a significant part of corporate life, and your involvement in culture and the arts provides the opportunity both to sponsor and to attend distinguished social events.

Sixth, because government leaders often have special cultural interests and favourite projects, your sponsorship of similar projects and causes provides the opportunity to form useful alliances and valuable contacts.

Seventh, corporate sponsorship of the arts is good for recruiting. From the mail I receive, it's clear that many bright young people are eager to work in a company that clearly cares about community and cultural concerns. I'm interested in these people because in my experience successful managers tend to be broad rather than narrow in their range of interests.

Eighth, in an era when corporations are often criticized for their alleged lack of social involvement, participation in cultural or arts programmes can present excellent opportunities to be involved in constructive social action. We at Mobil made this link with your Young Audiences programme. Because the prime beneficiaries of most corporate support for the arts – including our own – tend to be relatively affluent people, we established a programme that provided young people from minority groups with the opportunity to be exposed early in life to meaningful artistic experiences.

I recognize, of course, that most institutions are hardly in a position to undertake a venture on the grand scale of *Masterpiece Theatre*. But the advantages and benefits I have just cited apply equally to much smaller projects. Over the years, we at Mobil have initiated a number of more modest programmes; perhaps the brief list that follows may suggest some ideas and directions for other companies and organizations.

THE BICENTENNIAL POSTERS

In 1975, a year before the nation's bicentennial, we started looking for a project that would be visible, long-lasting, and inexpensive – or even, if possible, self-liquidating.

Somehow, I hit upon the idea of a series of posters. We came up with a theme – 'America, the Third Century' – and asked thirteen leading American artists each to produce one poster. Then we approached the Bicentennial Commission and convinced its members to designate these works as the official Bicentennial posters. By arranging their sale through art galleries and poster shops, we were able to recover all of our costs.

DOUBLE DUTCH

A few years ago, I received a call from Dave Walker, a New York City detective who described his idea for a double-dutch jump-rope competition for girls in the New York City school system. In 1973, the police department officially organized double dutch as a competitive sports programme; more recently, the programme has spread to other cities as well.

Mobil took an active role in helping to fund the programme, in developing a brochure to explain the rules, and in producing a training film. We also provided T-shirts and offered jump-rope clinics led by professional boxers and dancers. With an initial grant of only $7,500, we were able to help provide an exciting competitive programme for thousands of inner-city girls.

CONCERTS ON THE CANAL

Concerts on the Canal is a programme of free concerts – jazz, swing, bluegrass, and much more – on the Chesapeake & Ohio Canal in the Georgetown section of Washington, D.C. We started the programme in 1978, during a low point in the public's perception of oil companies. We chose Georgetown because it was the centre of Washington's political and social life.

We began with a grant of $7,000, which covered a whole season of concerts, as well as banners and a great deal of free publicity in the local media. The programme now costs $13,000 a year, which is stil a bargain price for a series of concerts that is attended by thousands of people and known about by many more.

THE BIG APPLE RELAYS

This is a one-day track-and-field event for high-school boys and girls living in the five boroughs of New York. We started the programme in 1980 with a grant of $2,000; today it's all the way up to $3,000.

THE PEGASUS ATHLETIC AWARD DINNERS

A few years ago, Bill Travers of the *New York Daily News* wrote a column asking why companies routinely honoured male athletes in New York public schools but did nothing for their female counterparts. Mobil took that question seriously, and we began sponsoring an annual dinner at Tavern on the Green, the famous Central Part restaurant, to honour the best performers in girls' athletics. The guests include the award winners, the finalists, representatives of the school system, the coaches, and the girls' parents. As always, there is plenty of local coverage. We started this programme in 1982 with a grant of $8,300; today, our annual expenditure is $14,000.

THE PEGASUS PRIZE FOR LITERATURE

Although this programme is barely known in the United States, the Pegasus Prize for Literature is an important and cost-effective multinational project whose purpose is to introduce American readers to distinguished fiction from countries whose national literature is rarely translated into English. The prize includes a monetary award, a medal, and translation and publication of the work. Each year, the winning book is translated into English and published by the Louisiana State University Press. This programme costa approximately $50,000 a year.

THE LIONS AT THE LIBRARY

In the mid-1970s, a newspaper article revealed that the two stone lions standing guard outside the main branch of the New York Public Library – their names, by the way, are Patience and Fortitude – were rapidly disintegrating as a result of chemicals in the air. The library estimated that it would cost $25,000 to save the lions. Because we are great admirers of the library, which is a couple of blocks from our office, we decided to pick up the cost of restoring the lions. During the restoration, there were big stories in the press, huge banners in front of the library, and a great deal of ongoing publicity until Patience and Fortitude were nursed back to health.

TUESDAY NIGHT AT THE MUSEUMS

For years, Mobil has been providing grants to major New York museums, including the Whitney, the Guggenheim, the Museum of Natural History, and others, which enable those institutions to stay open on Tuesday nights at no cost to the public. This is a tremendously cost-effective project, for, among other benefits, it enables us to attach our name to any exhibit – as in, 'Come and see the van Gogh exhibition free, courtesy of Mobil Oil.'

I especially like this project because it reaches out to the public and helps the museums at the same time – without encroaching in any way on their artistic autonomy. The museum projects are clearly more expensive than the others described here, but compared to the cost of underwriting a major exhibit, they're a bargain.

STUDENT FILMMAKERS
For the past ten years or so, we've been sponsoring a major West Coast competition for young filmmakers whereby they get to test themselves against their peers. The programme is cosponsored by the National Academy of Television Arts and Sciences, and it costs us approximately $50,000 a year.

THE MISSING CHILDREN PROGRAMME
In Washington, D.C., we recently became involved in a campaign to help locate missing children. The campaign, sponsored jointly by Mobil and the Acadia Group (a life-insurance company) is receiving a great deal of help from other businesses in the area – notably a local TV station, which broadcasts 'Missing Children Reports' on a daily basis. This programme, which costs us about $75,000, shows that there is no limit to the kinds of projects that a corporation can get involved in.

AFFINITY-OF-PURPOSE MARKETING

When we undertook to produce *Masterpiece Theatre*, as well as the various other projects I have just mentioned, we didn't give much thought to their ultimate effect on the bottom line. In financial terms, we took it for granted that these projects would cost us far more than they would return, but that they were worth doing for other reasons.

But times have changed. Today, after fifteen years of artistic and cultural activity, we now find that when we give certain publics a reason to identify with the projects and causes that we have chosen to support, they will translate that identification into a preference for doing business with us. Because this is a fairly recent development, let's take a moment to understand how and why it works.

For most companies, most of the time, the most effective way to increase sales has always been through conventional broad-based advertising. At the same time, a growing number of consumers are highly and deliberately resistant to product advertising. To them, most advertising is infantile, shallow, and misleading. Even the most successful commercials are offensive to some viewers – and while this group may be a distinct minority, that still leaves millions of people who would much rather see Alistair Cooke than Mr Dirt. Very often, the people in this group are upscale viewers with the discretionary dollars to buy, for example, premium gasoline for all three of their cars.

The assumption among this public is that while individual advertisements may differ, competing products are all pretty much the same. Moreover, assuming that they watch commercial television in the first place, the people in this group generally make use of both video cassette recorders and cable TV, both of which have dramatically affected their attitude towards commercials as well as their exposure to them. Viewers who have complained for years about annoying commercials are finally able to strike back, and many of them use their VCRs not to watch movies, but to see their favourite programmes on tape – without the commercials, which are eliminated by pressing the fast-forward button on the remote control.

And once viewers have watched television without commercials – whether it's public TV, rented cassettes, delayed viewing, or a premium cable channel – it's more difficult than ever for them to sit through product advertising. As a result, while conventional television programmes are still promising to be 'right back after this message,' fewer and fewer viewers are staying around to find out.

It's not surprising, then, that advertisers are starting to scramble and are searching for new places to place their messages. Not long ago, some New York taxis started carrying computer-generated advertising, and there are even reports of advertising appearing in toilet stalls. Presumably, there are limits even to bad taste. But the point is clear: advertisers can no longer count on the captive audiences that were once so readily available on television.

Clearly, it's not just a small group of effete snobs who are engaged in this rebellion. Nor is the problem limited to television. Even 'average' men and women in the supermarket aisles are becoming fed up with infantile advertising. According to a recent survey, most shoppers would like to wring the neck of Mr Whipple, that wimpy TV character who used to whine, 'Please don't squeeze the Charmin.'

But sophistication alone won't solve the problem. Remember those sexy ads for designer jeans a few years back? They resulted in a lot of attention, but much of that attention was negative and it created a serious backlash. What all of this shows is that despite the conventional wisdom of corporate America, not all advertising is worth doing. In his classic work, *Ogilvy on Advertising*, David Ogilvy tells of a former head of marketing research at Ford who once ran insert ads in every copy of *Reader's Digest*. At the end of the year, he found that people who had not been exposed to the ad actually bought more Ford products than those who had.

In another survey cited by Ogilvy, it was found that consumption of a certain brand of beer was actually lower among people who had remembered its advertising than among those who did not. In other words, the brewer had spent millions of dollars on advertising that had *unsold* his beer.

As conventional advertising runs up against a growing number of obstacles, corporations are quickly discovering that one alternative to the various problems of traditional advertising is 'cause-related marketing' – also known as 'affinity-of-purpose marketing' – which consists of identifying your company with a worthy cause that a high proportion of your target sales audience happens to believe in. As a result of that identification, consumers reward you by buying your product or otherwise helping your business. In other words, they are choosing to help a third party by doing business with a second party.

Some companies practise cause-related marketing by linking their product to a specific cause or project: every time you buy one of their widgets, for example, they'll donate a dollar to the Fund for the Arts. We at Mobil prefer to practise this kind of marketing in a more general way, rather than tying it to a specific sale. But however it's done, it's clear that cause-related marketing is a valuable new tool for a new era. Incidentally, this is a technique that would not have worked during the antibusiness climate of 1965 to 1980; back then, it would have been viewed cynically as a cooption on the part of big business. But for the 1980s, it's an increasingly valuable adjunct to traditional advertising.

Affinity-of-purpose marketing is especially effective in promoting products (such as gasoline) or services (such as banking or airlines) that seem, on the surface, to be identical to what the competition has to offer. Traditionally, product advertising has stressed the unique aspects of a particular product. But a growing number of consumers are becoming aware that this much-vaunted 'uniqueness' is often only a mirage created by an ad agency. As a result, advertisers must find another way to differentiate their product from everybody else's. For a small but significant portion of the population, the answer is cause-related marketing.

The consumers who are reached by affinity-of-purpose marketing are not always motivated by lower prices, convenience, or gimmicks like trading stamps. As we've already seen, they're increasingly resistant to advertising. But very often, they can be reached through an intangible value such as social responsibility.

To be sure, cause-related marketing is not without its risks. After one of our op-ed messages applauded the recommendation of the Grace Commission that military commissaries be made more cost-efficient as one way of reducing the federal deficit, a hundred and fifty people protested by sending us their torn-up Mobil credit cards. We've also received protest letters from fundamentalists who felt that our *Life on Earth* and *Living Planet* television series were guilty of endorsing evolution.

While we don't relish the idea of losing even one customer, it's important to keep in mind that no activity will please 100 per cent of the public. The easiest way to offend nobody is to do nothing – which would leave all the positive opportunities to our competitors. So we'll continue to do what works so well.

Besides, how many people are buying Mobil products *because* of our ads and our underwriting? And how many thousands of homes and schools associate our name with quality programming? When we ran *Nicholas Nickleby* on television a few years back, some people actually sent us money to show their appreciation for what they had received for free.

There's no question that among certain groups cause-related marketing can be enormously effective. Back in 1982, Mobil commissioned a public-opinion survey of three hundred upscale college graduates in the Boston area. Since the study was conducted in Harvard's backyard, it came as no surprise that many of the respondents didn't agree with us on the issues. But they certainly knew who we were. When asked which company came to mind in connection with advocacy advertising, five times as many people said Mobil as second-place Exxon. Asked which company was identified with quality TV programming, people again chose Mobil by a large margin – even though Exxon spends much more money than we do. In fact, we often get letters thanking us for Exxon's programmes!

But the survey's finding that pleased us the most was that 31 per cent of these upscale respondents said they bought Mobil gasoline most often, compared to 16 per cent for Exxon, 15 per cent for Gulf, and 10 per cent for Texaco. Tubby Harrison, our pollster, was so surprised by these numbers that he wrote in the margin, 'Mobil must be the thinking man's gasoline.'

Cause-related marketing has been a motivation for our stockholders, too. Whenever we survey new shareholders, they generally give the usual investment reasons for buying our stock. But 9 per cent of the new shareholders name our public-issue ads, and 7 per cent cite our sponsorship of quality shows on public television. I find it amazing that so many of our new shareholders are willing to trust us with their money because of some discretionary cause or activity in which Mobil is engaged.

Now I don't mean to imply, of course, that we at Mobil invented cause-related marketing, or that we're the only corporation in America that's using it. Consider the case of American Express, and their recent campaign to allocate one cent of each dollar received from credit-card billings and traveller's-cheque fees to the Statue of Liberty restoration project. After all, major credit cards and traveller's cheques are all pretty much the same. But during the three months that this campaign ran, card-members' dollar charges on their American Express cards actually rose 30 per cent, while the number of cards grew by 15 per cent.

Another recent example of cause-related marketing was the programme undertaken by Budweiser urging donations to help fight muscular dystrophy. Not only did the effort raise some $12 million, but while the campaign was on, many supermarkets gave their prized end-space on shelves to six-packs of Bud.

In the fall of 1985, General Foods undertook a similar campaign. The company placed coupons in newspapers for Tang, its breakfast drink. For every coupon redeemed, General Foods promised to donate ten cents to Mothers Against Drunk Driving. Moreover, the company guaranteed that MADD would receive no less than $100,000 from the campaign.

None of these new developments mean that traditional advertising is dead, or that it is no longer effective for broad-based marketing. Far from it. But it is clear that we're entering a new area, in which people will base their buying judgments on a wider group of criteria. In this context, cause-related marketing is not only a cost-effective way to market to certain groups – it's downright cheap. And while we certainly didn't undertake our discretionary programmes with this particular advantage in mind, we're more than happy to reap the rewards.

MASTERPIECE THEATRE

Which brings us, finally, to the case of *Masterpiece Theatre*. On January 10, 1971, television viewers across the land heard a proper and distinguished English announcer inform them that the programme they were about to see was made possible by a grant from Mobil. None of us who were connected with the enterprise ever dreamed that the innocuous phrase that preceded the show would soon enter the language, or that over the years it would actually be the subject of cartoons in *The New Yorker*.

Back in 1970, when public television was just beginning to hit its stride, we at Mobil sat up and took notice. We believed that this new entity was going to become very important in American cultural life, and we were eager to be associated with it. We wanted to be helpful to public television, and we had a feeling that public television could be equally helpful to us.

While we had provided some early funding for *Sesame Street*, we were particularly interested in quality TV programming for adults. One day, I received a call from Stan Calderwood, the president of WGBH-TV, a public television station in Boston. Calderwood began by asking if I had been watching *The Forsyte Saga*, a BBC mini-series, on PBS. Now in those days – and I suppose the same holds true today – even those people who didn't watch serious drama on public television would usually say that they did. So although I had never seen a single episode, I assured Stan Calderwood that *The Forsyte Saga* was one of my favourite shows.

In that case, Calderwood said, I might be interested in the fact that Mobil could purchase thirty-nine hours of BBC television drama for $390,000 – which came out to $10,000 an hour. Even in 1970, that was an absurdly low figure for television, so I was eager to learn more. At the time, I had no idea that Calderwood had already made the same offer to at least fifty other corporations, all of whom had turned him down.

At the urging of our top leadership, I flew over to London with Frank Marshall, a public-relations consultant with considerable experience in quality television. Frank and I spent a week cooped up in a screening room, and while I no longer recall the specific programmes we saw, I vividly remember how enormously impressed and excited we were.

A few weeks later, the deal was made. Mobil called a press conference to announce a million-dollar commitment to public television – in particular, *Sesame Street*, for children, and, for adults, a new show called *Masterpiece Theatre*, consisting of a series of English dramas. At the time, this was the largest grant of its kind, and our gift received a great deal of publicity. Until then, most of the funding for public television came from the Ford Foundation.

Our working arrangement for *Masterpiece Theatre* has always been with WGBH-TV in Boston, which, in the language of television, serves as the 'station of entry.' While WGBH has the final say on programme selection, we provide the leadership on advertising, promotion, and publicity.

Originally, 'Masterpiece Theatre' was merely our working title, the assumption being that we'd soon come up with a better one. We never did. In fact, the only real disagreement over the title had to do with how to spell *theater*. Christopher Sarson, the original producer of *Masterpiece Theatre* at WGBH, insisted on the British spelling, as did his colleagues at the station. I thought that was a big pretentious, but Sarson's view prevailed.

But while I didn't agree with Christopher Sarson's spelling preference, I certainly couldn't argue with his choice of the theme music. Years earlier, Chris and his wife were on a Club Med vacation where the guests were awakened each morning by the majestic strains of 'Fanfare for the King's Supper' by J. J. Mouret. Chris fell in love with the piece and made a mental note to use it someday for a TV show. Because 'Fanfare' was composed in France, he assumed, at first, that it couldn't be used for a series of shows from England. But no other music he could find sounded so right, so he went ahead with it anyway.

Now we needed a host. Alistair Cooke already enjoyed a fine reputation for interpreting American culture to English audiences, so it seemed reasonable to expect that he could do the same in reverse. In addition, Cooke had extensive experience in television. Throughout the 1950s, he had served as master of ceremonies for the very popular *Omnibus*, a sophisticated Sunday-afternoon television magazine programme of arts and entertainment. More recently, he has hosted *Alistair Cooke's America*.

But when Christopher Sarson first approached Cooke about taking the job, Cooke turned him down. 'The person you need,' Alistair Cooke said with his customary eloquence, 'is somebody with the artful offhandedness of Max Beerbohm, the zest of John Mason Brown, or the talkative guile of Alexander Woollcott.'

'You're so right,' said Sarson. 'But there's one problem with the people you mentioned. They're all dead.'

Cooke had no reply, and the job was his.

When it came time to promote *The First Churchills*, which was our initial offering on *Masterpiece Theatre*, we weren't exactly sure how to proceed. To announce the series, our advertising agency came up with a large-print ad that focused on our million-dollar grant. Over a huge photograph of Rawleigh Warner was a headline that read 'The Chairman of Mobil Oil is an Angel.'

When I saw that, I hit the roof. Not only was the ad completely wrong for the kind of show we wanted to present, but it also violated one of my cardinal principles – that you should never attempt to tell the world how great you are. For better or worse, that's a decision that people have to make on their own.

A week later, the agency came back with a new ad, whose headline read 'Mobil has De-Boobed the Tube.' If anything, this one was worse. Not only were we bragging, but this time we were also undercutting the intellectual image we had worked so hard to achieve.

Finally, we came up with our own idea. This time, the ad featured a large picture of Susan Hampshire as the Duchess of Marlborough, accompanied by the headline 'Winston Churchill's Great Great Great Great Grandmother.' Now *that* was more like it.

The early reactions to *Masterpiece Theatre* were extraordinary. Millions of viewers felt enriched and ennobled, and hundreds of thousands soon became *Masterpiece Theatre* fanatics. The critics, too, were enthusiastic, hailing the new programme as the kind of television that culture-starved viewers had been waiting for. Despite the sceptics who believed that the American viewing public wanted nothing more challenging than cop shows and situation comedies, we established that there was, indeed, an audience for quality television – and, better yet, that it could be presented for a relatively modest price.

Throughout the history of *Masterpiece Theatre*, there has been a degree of resentment among American actors that all of the shows have been made in England. We have been attacked several times by the Screen Actors Guild, and by Ed Asner, its president, for relying on imported productions and not supporting local talent.

Our critics, apparently, would prefer that we practise some form of protectionism or intellectual isolationism. But we at Mobil believe in the free-market system – for television and everything else. Besides, the protectionists overlook a very important fact that undermines their argument. When it comes to television, what America imports from other countries can't even begin to compare in volume with the staggering amount of television that we sell to the rest of the world – including England.

When we buy television programmes, our decisions are based on only two criteria: quality and price. Unfortunately, in our experience, the American television industry isn't competitive in either respect.

Some people are surprised to learn that price matters to us as much as quality. Because Mobil is one of the largest companies in the world, they assume that we must have unlimited resources behind every project we undertake. While I wish that were so, our real situation is far more mundane. After all, we are not in the communications business. Our support for public television comes out of our discretionary funds, so it is especially important that we get as much for our dollar as we possibly can.

And there's no question that our dollar goes much farther in England. Among other considerations, the English entertainment industry has less powerful unions, lower salaries, and a more work-oriented spirit. In 1984, when Michael Grade was appointed head of programming for the main channel of the BBC, he was asked if he had learned anything during his two years in Hollywood as president of Embassy Television (Norman Lear's production company) that he was going to bring back to England.

'Yes,' he replied. 'I'm going to introduce valet parking.'

But even if we could afford to buy American-made shows, would they be as good as what we buy in England? While there's no question that Hollywood is still capable of making great movies, *Masterpiece Theatre* does not acquire movies. What we look for is theatre that works on television. Unfortunately, there is very little theatrical television being made in America that can compete with the quality of the British programmes that we buy.

While the first three years of *Masterpiece Theatre* were highly successful, it was with *Upstairs, Downstairs* in 1974, that we achieved a breakthrough to a mass audience. I first learned about the show from Rawleigh Warner, Jr., who had been told about it by the Duchess of Bedford at a dinner party in London. Frank Marshall and I saw a few episodes, and we thought it was wonderful.

Unfortunately, the people at WGBH did not agree. *Upstairs, Downstairs*, the story of the Bellamy family and their servants – the inhabitants of a single house in the Belgravia section of London during the first three decades of the twentieth century – was completely different from anything else that *Masterpiece Theatre* had ever offered. It wasn't high culture. It wasn't drawn from a novel. To make matters worse, it was in some respects – horror of horrors – a soap opera.

When at first I was unable to convince WGBH to feature *Upstairs, Downstairs* on *Masterpiece Theatre*, I told the station that I was going to buy it anyway. 'When this show is promoted properly,' I declared, 'the public will see it for what it is – an intelligent and witty commentary on the class system, and a great entertainment.' In the end, after much argument, WGBH gave in.

Clearly, it was the split-level sociology of the story that made the show so popular. In addition to the fascinating double perspective, there was also the curiosity factor: no matter which side the audience identified with, each group was eager to see how the other half lived. Within a couple of years, American tourists were seen wandering up and down Eaton Place, just off Belgravia Square looking in vain for number 165 – much as earlier generations of tourists had searched on Baker Street for the house where Sherlock Holmes had once smoked his famous meerschaum pipe.

As good as some of the shows have been, the success of *Masterpiece Theatre* depends upon a great deal of behind-the-scenes work. Every time we make a decision to acquire a new show, for example, we immediately initiate a graphic concept that will be used in all of our ads, on posters, and on the cover of the press kit. Coming up with the right illustration is not always easy; for *The Jewel in the Crown* we went through six different designs before settling on a drawing of scenes from India with the three main characters in the foreground. (The original drawing had depicted a peacock and a jewel, and while it was stunning, it said nothing about the characters or the story.)

While the graphic artist is working on the design, the public-relations firm of Frank Goodman begins to work on the press materials. We use an outside PR firm because Frank Goodman, an old-fashioned press agent with years of experience in theatre, knows more about television publicity than anybody else in the business.

After seeing the show on cassettes, Frank and his staff go off to London to interview the director, the screenwriter, and the principal actors. They learn everything they can about how the show was made, and they produce a series of short articles and photographs, which they send to American newspapers and magazines.

To take a recent example, the first episode of *The Jewel in the Crown* aired on public television stations on December 16, 1984. Eight months earlier, Frank Goodman and his staff had gone to London to conduct a series of interviews. During the summer, five months before the show was to air, they started sending cassettes to key people in the media, and to selected critics – including John Leonard of *New York* magazine. Leonard promptly wrote a review, which included his assessment that '*The Jewel in the Crown* is the best sustained television I've seen in more than 30 years of watching.'

When Leonard's review appeared, we knew that we had a major hit on our hands. For when it come to quality television, the print reviews are especially important. While there is a loyal group of viewers who watch a great deal of public television, a successful PBS show must draw two other groups of viewers: those who normally watch only the commercial networks, and those who normally don't watch television at all. In general, the latter group will take the trouble to watch *Masterpiece Theatre* if they've read something good about it in a newspaper or magazine. It is for their sake that one of our press releases describes *Masterpiece Theatre* as 'intelligent television for people who don't ordinarily watch television.'

Incidentally, one expected bonus of *Masterpiece Theatre* has been that the various books our shows have been based on, which have often been forgotten or virtually ignored, have enjoyed a sudden rush of popularity. So much for the popular myth that television leads people to stop reading! In this case, as Alistair Cooke once pointed out, the old injunction was reversed, so that now the slogan might be reformulated: 'You saw the movie, now read the book.'

In October 1984, two months before *Jewel* went on the air, we brought television critics from all over the country to New York to preview the series, and to meet two special guests – Dame Peggy Ashcroft, who was part of the brilliant cast, and Sir Denis Forman, the chairman of Granada Television, which had produced the series.

Sir Denis, who had been stationed in India during World War Two – Paul Scott, who wrote the book, was there during the same period, although the two never met – was the motivating force behind *The Jewel in the Crown*, an immense project that involved the tranformation of four novels about the British rule in India into fourteen hours of television. For years, visitors to Forman's office would see the pages of Scott's novel tacked to the walls, as Sir Denis worked feverishly to make the long and complex plot of the books suitable for a television series.

Frank Goodman was convinced that Sir Denis should fly to America to meet with the American critics, but Sir Denis was reluctant.

'Why should I go?' he asked Frank.

Frank took a deep breath. 'Because if you don't,' he said, 'everybody in the States will think this show was made by the BBC.' That did it.

Sir Denis turned out to be a highly quotable fellow. 'It's easy to make bad programmes,' he said. 'It's also easy to make good programmes that nobody wants to see. The trick is to make popular programmes that are also good.'

And: 'Always underestimate the public's knowledge of a subject, but never underestimate their intelligence.'

HOW TO FUND PUBLIC TELEVISION

In my view, noncommercial television ought to be supported by the people and the institutions who believe in it. That's why our tag line on *Masterpiece Theatre* is 'Made possible by a grant from Mobil Corporation, which invites you to join with them in supporting public television.'

While public television is enormously important to our society, I am opposed to its receiving any money from the government. For one thing, whenever the government becomes involved in supporting the arts and culture, the decision-making apparatus inevitably becomes politicized. For another, much of the money that is funnelled into the arts and culture never reaches the people who are the creators. Instead, it tends to go to hired bureaucrats whose job it is to make artistic decisions about how the taxpayers' money should be spent.

If our society is determined that the government should help to support the arts and culture, a bloated and politicized arts bureaucracy is the wrong way to go about it. A far better way to proceed is by having the government issue the cultural equivalent of food stamps. I mean this seriously: The government could establish that below a certain income level, people would be issued vouchers that could be used for any artistic or cultural event of their choice. Each theatre, symphony, or moviehouse would then send the vouchers to Washington for redemption. The advantage to this system is that it would eliminate the culture brokers and would support the arts in a democratic way by letting the people, rather than the bureaucrats, decide where the money should go.

Under this new system, a person could certainly choose to spend some of his vouchers to support public television. But I don't believe that public television should be a privileged recipient of government funds. Whenever I'm addressing an audience and this topic comes up, I always ask: How many people in this room support government funding for PBS? Invariably, most people raise their hands. Then I ask: How many people think that the government should start publishing a daily newspaper? Whereupon all of the hands immediately go down. Predictably, the group's First Amendment sensitivities are offended by the very idea of a government newspaper. But if a government-supported newspaper is objectionable, why is there no outcry against government-supported television?

In the absence of a cultural-voucher system, and without any other form of government support, where will public television (and public radio, for that matter) find the millions of dollars that are necessary to keep it alive as a quality alternative to the commercial stations and networks? Beyond the current sources – the actual and potential money that can be raised from individuals, corporations, foundations, and labour unions – there is a logical source of additional funds. As everybody knows, there are thousands of commercial television and radio stations across the land that have been licensed by the government, through the FCC, to operate on a particular channel in a particular market. While these stations have to satisfy certain minimum requirements to be granted that licence, they pay no fee for the monopoly they enjoy. If it were up to me, there would be a special licence fee through which commercial stations would help to subsidize public radio and television.

If they were presented with this proposal, the commercial stations and the networks that service them would undoubtedly argue that they already pay taxes, just like every other business. So why should they be singled out for this additional payment?

But the fact is that many industries pay special fees for the use of public facilities, fees that are set aside for particular purposes. Truckers pay an extra fee for using the highways. Airlines pay for using airports. The oil industry pays special fees for the opportunity to look for oil on federal lands. In fact, the broadcasting industry is the only one I can think of that uses a public-owned asset – the airwaves – at no cost.

When you stop to consider that a company operating a concession stand at Yosemite Park has to pay a fee to the government, you begin to wonder: from an economic point of view, how is publicly owned land different from the publicly owned airwaves?

It's abundantly clear that the use of the airwaves has become a very profitable operation for certain companies and their shareholders. In recent months, we have seen the transfer of licences from one private owner to another in return for hundreds of millions of dollars – not to mention the historic acquisition of ABC by Capital Cities. Now I'm not for a moment suggesting that the government should take over the operation of these companies, any more than I would want to see a government oil agency empowered to search for oil on federal lands. But it just isn't right for the broadcast industry to make money from a public facility without paying for that privilege.

Based on a percentage of their profits, or perhaps on the size of their market, every individual station should pay an annual fee that would be placed in a trust fund to support public television and public radio. So instead of government funding, public television would benefit from government-enforced private financing. It's a good compromise, and it would ensure the smooth functioning of one of our most important public institutions.

But to return to our broader subject, it's clear to me, based on fifteen years of hard experience, that supporting cultural activities involves far more than that nice, warm feeling of having done the right thing. As we have seen, this kind of activity is beneficial on several fronts, including employee morale, the enhanced visibility of top leadership, recruiting, and projecting the image of a responsible and active corporation that is concerned with excellence. Finally, your support on culture and the arts can pay off in increased profits – especially among groups that are difficult to reach in more convenient ways. Which supports what I've always believed anyway – that public relations is advertising by other means.

NINE

Achieving a Distinctive Personality

ANYONE WHO LOOKS AT successful individuals and successful corporations will immediately see what both groups have in common: a distinctive personality, or, if you prefer, a distinctive style. Throughout this book, I have tried to provide some guidelines for achieving distinctiveness in a substantive sense, whether the task at hand is dealing with the press, engaged in confrontations with other organizations, getting your views heard in Washington, or dealing with the public in other ways.

Distinctiveness depends not only on what you do, but on how you do it. During the course of this book, I have offered a number of principles and plenty of advice on how to get the job done. In this final chapter, I want to embellish those remarks with a few operating principles having to do with achieving a distinctive style both for your organization – through the projects it undertakes – and for you as a corporate leader.

CREATING A DISTINCTIVE CORPORATE STYLE

• *Being loved is not your objective.* Too many institutions undertake their projects with no real objective other than a vague desire to attract an amorphous quality known as 'goodwill.' Now there's nothing inherently wrong with generating goodwill; it's just that by itself, goodwill doesn't help you very much. If your only purpose is to get people to love you, then why bother? Is that amorphous 'love' really useful from a corporate point of view? The institution that blindly accumulates goodwill is like the gambler who wins a pile of chips in a casino and never bothers to cash them in.

But while some companies act in order to be loved, others don't even have that as a goal. Before you undertake any project, be sure you understand why you're doing it. Being respected is one reasonable objective for an institution; being understood is another. And so is being a participant in the debate over a major issue. But being loved is not, in my view, a compelling or useful objective for a corporation.

Individual programmes, of course, may have more limited goals. You may be interested in boosting employee morale. You might want to enhance your image for purposes of recruitment. You might want to protect the interests of shareholders. You might want to improve your relations with government officials, or with the press, or with intellectuals, or with any other segment of the larger public.

On the other hand, your motivation for a particular project may arise out of a pure desire to be philanthropic. You may want to support and call attention to a good cause simply because it's a good cause and deserves support. You may be interested in helping to support culture and the arts. Your institution may decide to support any number of projects that are fundamenally decent, or kind, or valuable to society. You should become involved in these projects because they're worth supporting for their own sake, and not because you want to be loved.

Dale Carnegie was too simplistic. While winning friends and influencing people are both worth doing, they often require very different – and sometimes even mutually exclusive – techniques. When you're faced with a choice, your goal should be to influence people.

• *Don't try to duplicate somebody else's project.* You can't achieve significant attention or success by imitating other people's achievements. If you're going to undertake a project, make sure that it's fresh, different, and, above all, appropriate to your company's personality and values.

• *Never share the sponsorship of a project.* No matter how limited your budget may be, spend it on projects that can be identified exclusively with your company. Becoming a joint sponsor is usually a waste of your money. Instead of sharing a larger project, it's far better to be the sole sponsor of a smaller one.

There are several reasons for this. First, if a project has several sponsors, journalists may find it easier not to mention any of you by name. From their perspective, it's far easier to refer to the coalition than to mention all of the partners.

Second, it's very difficult to do ancillary promotion for a project if every idea you want to act on must first be cleared with your cosponsors. Committees are not known for either creativity or efficiency.

Third, if you're in a group with sponsors who are better known or bigger than you are, it's they who will receive most of the attention. And if the other sponsors are smaller than you, then you're needlessly diluting your efforts.

Still, there may be times when you have little choice but to share the sponsorship of a programme. When that happens, be sure that the people or the groups you're working with have an excellent reputation. In business, as in your personal life, you will be known by the company you keep.

• *Don't look back.* Once you've decided to embark on a programme, ride it for all its worth. Don't be halfhearted, and don't worry if at first you seem to be on the wrong course. If you start expressing doubts, your ambivalence will be contagious; before you know it, you will have created a self-fulfilling prophecy. If you have doubts or reservations about a project, be sure to resolve them before you begin.

• *Don't succumb to the sin of pride.* If you think your project is successful, don't tell a soul; if you're right, you won't need to. Most people resent bragging, even when it's justified. And most people don't like to have their judgments made for them; they'd much rather arrive at conclusions on their own. If you're constantly telling people how great your project is, even if you're right, both you and your project will be diminished in their eyes.

The same principle holds true in your own organization. Over the years, some of my colleagues have urged me to send press clippings about our projects to top management and to the members of the board. I've generally refused to do this because the real success, in my view, comes when these people see the press coverage on their own, or when they hear about our programmes from an outside source. If your project is a winner, you won't need to point that out. And if it isn't, your bragging won't fool anyone.

CREATING A DISTINCTIVE PERSONAL STYLE

• *Don't be a corporate type.* To the public, corporations and the people who run them often seem wooden and predictable. It's bad enough that many institutions have no apparent personality; you don't have to magnify the problem by suppressing your own. Think of the people you admire professionally; chances are that they all have a distinctive personal style. Why is Lee Iacocca of Chrysler the spokesman for the auto industry, even though Ford and General Motors are much larger companies? It's because the real leaders in any society are not afraid of showing who they are. So be yourself, and don't let your job define your personality.

This doesn't mean, of course, that you should take on somebody else's manner or personality – even if it's somebody you admire. If you imitate another person's distinctive style, that style is no longer distinctive.

A large part of your style is reflected in the way you speak. If you talk just like everybody else – or worse, like a corporate type is expected to talk – you won't be very effective. Consider this response from a corporate person in trouble: 'My associates and I have been unfairly maligned by these pernicious allegations. We are confident, at this point in time, that when the true facts have been made apparent, the aforesaid allegations will be shown to constitute a wholly unfounded assault on the integrity of the organization.' Honestly, would you pay attention to anyone who talked like that?

• *Show up early to meetings.* Some people think that coming late to a meeting makes them seem important. In reality, however, it only makes them look like they want to seem important. Arriving five minutes early for a meeting increases your confidence, helps you get comfortable, and gives you a slight edge over those who arrive after the meeting has begun. Leave early, if you must, but don't arrive late.

• *Answer your own telephone.* Answer your own phone whenever you can – especially if your job involves regular contact with the public or press. For one thing, it's more efficient: if you don't take the call now, you'll have to return it later, when the person who called you may not be around. Second, answering your own phone shows that you're a real person and that you're approachable.

The press likes to complain that people who work for large corporations are impossible to reach, so I always enjoy it when they find me on the first try. 'Do you really answer your own phone?' they ask in amazement.

'Absolutely,' I reply. 'Other people here have *important* things to do.'

By the same token, you should also place your own calls. Having your secretary do this for you is actually less efficient, because it ties you both up.

But here's where I draw the line: There's nothing I hate more than picking up the phone to hear a voice saying, 'Please hold for Mr Smith,' followed by a long silence. Whenever that happens, I look at my watch and give Smith exactly twenty-five seconds to start talking. If he hasn't come on the line by then, I hang up.

Invariably, Smith's secretary calls back a moment later. 'I'm sorry,' she says, 'we were cut off.'

'No we weren't,' I always reply. 'I hung up.'

• *Give every caller two minutes.* I'll talk to anybody for two minutes, because I've learned that when people call me – especially if they want to pitch an idea – they don't necessarily expect to be successful. All they really want is a chance to make their best pitch to the person who makes the decisions.

'I'll need to see something in writing,' I usually say, 'but tell me a little about it now.' If the project is probably not for us, I'll say so, but I'll still invite the caller to put it in writing so we can look at it more closely.

I see three advantages to taking every call. First, there's always the possibility that I'll learn something useful. Second, even if the call turns out to be a waste of my time, at least I was able to be both accessible and polite to the caller. Third, there's always the chance that somebody might give me a great opportunity. Admittedly, it doesn't happen very often, but *Masterpiece Theatre* originated with a phone call from someone I didn't know.

• *Always ask questions.* Remember what the teacher told you on your first day of school? 'If there's anything you don't understand, just raise your hand and ask.' That was good advice, and it still holds true. You no longer have to raise your hand, but your willingness to ask questions is the key to increasing both your awareness and your knowledge – which will, in turn, improve your efficiency.

Asking good, penetrating questions may be the most important thing that a manager can do. And yet a great many executives never do it. Perhaps they feel that asking questions will make them feel foolish. Or perhaps they want to give other people the impression that they already know it all.

If you don't ask questions, you're probably making important decisions in a vacuum. Even worse, you may be accepting other people's reports and recommendations at face value. You probably don't like to see yourself as naive, but the manager who is afraid to ask questions can rarely attain a high level of sophistication.

How do you know what questions to ask? First, you must overcome your fear of asking the wrong ones. You will, occasionally, ask a stupid question. And while that may lead to some momentary embarrassment, you will have learned something important that you should have known all along. Better now than later – or never.

A second good rule about questions is to put yourself in the other guy's position. Think about your boss, for example; what would he want to know about this programme? How about a legislator? Or a journalist?

Finally, you should ask questions of anyone who presumes to give you answers. I often find myself in situations in which somebody says that I 'must' take a certain course of action. Whenever I hear that word, I always ask: 'And what will happen if I don't?'

• *Be aware of where your power comes from.* Never allow yourself to forget that no matter how bright or talented you may be, virtually all of your power and prestige emanate not from you but from the institution you work for. This is a special occupational hazard for television anchormen, who are the objects of so much corporate flattery that they almost invariably come to believe that they're uniquely intelligent, talented, and powerful. But on another level, all corporate executives must deal with this temptation. It's relatively easy to start believing your own clippings; don't do it.

Because it's very difficult to keep yourself honest, it's important that you hire people who have the courage – and the freedom – to help you out in that process.

• *Be a good leader.* I can think of at least six qualities that characterize a good leader. First, a good leader is always willing to do the dirty work. He'll sweep out the store if that's what's required to make a project succeed. If everyone on the team has to make a sacrifice, he'll set an example for the others to follow.

Second, a good leader isn't afraid to hire people who are smarter or more creative than himself. He knows that if he goes to the usual mediocre sources, he's going to end up with the usual mediocre results. A real leader can harness the energy of creative people in a way that will enhance the entire enterprise.

Third, a good leader is enthusiastic during tough times. Leaders who constantly complain about a bad situation can rarely motivate the troops and help them to overcome adversity. In a crisis, optimism and confidence are even more important than experience and intelligence.

Fourth, a good leader has vision. In my experience, there are two kinds of leaders – the 'let's-nots, and the 'why-nots.' When times are tough, the let's-nots prefer to retreat, to stay with the familiar, to avoid taking risks. The why-nots, on the other hand, are open to fresh ideas and bold possibilities. If the old answers don't work, they're willing to experiment with new and unconventional solutions.

Fifth, a good leader is tough – a quality that has to do less with personality than with character. It's not that the tough leader is abrasive, or uncaring, or insensitive. It's simply that he's willing and able to make difficult or unpopular decisions – and to live with their consequences.

Finally, a good leader holds a set of philosophical principles that guide him when it comes to specific issues. Rather than making every decision on an ad hoc basis, he has formed some conlusions about the basic objectives of his corporation and about how those objectives should be reached. By the same token, he knows that the long-term health and survival of the corporation must always take precedence over short-term gains.

Let me conclude with a bit of wisdom from Rabbi Hillel, whom I think of as the patron saint of creative confrontation. The rabbi said: 'If I am not for myself, who will be for me? But if I am only for myself, what am I?'